BERLITZ®

MONTREAL

1989/1990 Edition

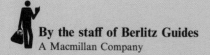

By the staff of Berlitz Guides
A Macmillan Company

Library of Congress Catalog Card Number:
76-21373.

Berlitz Trademark Reg. U.S. Patent Office
and other countries—Marca Registrada

Printed in Switzerland by Weber SA, Bienne

8th Printing
1989/1990 Edition

How to use our guide

- All the practical information, hints and tips that you will need before and during the trip start on page 100.

- For general background, see the sections The City and the People, p. 6, and A Brief History, p. 12.

- All the sights to see are listed between pages 23 and 55, with suggestions for daytrips from Montreal described on pages 56 to 71. Our own choice of sights most highly recommended is pinpointed by the Berlitz traveler symbol.

- Entertainment, nightlife and all other leisure activities are described between pages 72 and 89, while information on restaurants and cuisine is to be found on pages 90 to 99.

- Finally, there is an index at the back of the book, pp. 126–128.

Although we make every effort to ensure the accuracy of all the information in this book, changes occur incessantly. We cannot therefore take responsibility for facts, prices, addresses and circumstances in general that are constantly subject to alteration. Our guides are updated on a regular basis as we reprint, and we are always grateful to readers who let us know of any errors, changes or serious omissions they come across.

Text: Tom Brosnahan
Photography: Ted Grant
Layout: Doris Haldemann
We are particularly grateful to Christine Curchod, V. Arlene Gaunt, V.M. Nicholson and David Pulman for their help in the preparation of this book. We also wish to thank the Canadian Government Office of Tourism and Direction Générale du Tourisme du Québec for their invaluable assistance.

4 Cartography: Falk-Verlag, Hamburg

Contents

The City and the People

Mont Réal—the Royal Mountain, the largest French-speaking city in the world outside of Paris, yet less than 50 miles from the border of New York State. Surrounded by urban bustle, with towering office blocks soaring above a grid of downtown streets, the city stands proud, with the mountain at its heart, protecting its history.

At this spot lay the enchanting natural beauty shared by the Algonquin, the Mohawk, the Iroquois. Here is where the Indians established their settlement of Hochelaga visited by Jacques Cartier in 1535, and here is where you'll see the gigantic cross commemorating the time when Maisonneuve arrived to colonize and spread the Catholic faith among the Indians.

With its soul rooted in 400 years of history, Montreal today is one of North America's most progressive and exciting cities. Mirabel Airport is the world's largest, surpassing even the giant Texan aerodrome of Dallas-Fort Worth. The Montreal Metro system speeds you along on noiseless rubber wheels to destinations like Man

and His World, the Olympic Park and Place Ville-Marie, starting point for a stroll through the fabulous Underground City. After that, you can take a boat out onto the river to marvel at one of man's greatest engineering feats—the St. Lawrence Seaway—and return to wander the streets of one of the best preserved old towns on the continent, Vieux Montréal.

If religion inspired the first European settlers in the area,

furs, timber, abundant game, fertile land and good river transport soon attracted many more—making the land a rich prize for a conqueror. And so it was; in 1760 British troops had wrenched it from the French and were marching in the streets of Montreal.

Thus, the city is the child of three ancestors: its Indian natives, its French founders and its British governors. The 200-year-old debate still goes on as to who has done the most for the city.

Of the 3 million Canadians who live in Greater Montreal, about two-thirds speak French as their first language, about

Real Quebecer? Or part French, Irish, Greek, or Central European? In the faces of many Montrealers features of parents' homelands are visible.

a quarter were brought up speaking English. But though most Montrealers know some of each, they're not always sure whether to ask for a *chien chaud* for lunch, or a hot dog; and is it *a* hot dog or *un* hot-dog? And where's the best place to have it, in a sidewalk café or a pub?

Summer in Place Ville-Marie contrasts strikingly with winter fun on Beaver Lake, Mount Royal.

Adding to the variety of the city are immigrants from the world over, for this is a truly cosmopolitan town, where Italians and Germans have a weekly newspaper, Arabs a cultural center, Hindus a radio program. And yet all are Montrealers; all delight in a glass of fine cider, "the wine of Quebec," and in a plate of steaming *fèves au lard* (pork and beans) to fend off winter's chill.

And winter is part of the secret of Montreal. The citizens live under thick snow for several months of every year. The demanding climate brings them together, makes them special. In February the newspaper advertisements tempt many with invitations to sunny Florida, but most would never think of abandoning their city with so much going on: theater and concerts at the Place des Arts, toboggan rides down the slopes of Mount Royal, skiing and snowshoeing in the Laurentian mountains. Besides, who wants to leave town when the hockey season's at its height?

Winter is also work-time, when bankers set investment schedules, lights burn late in university laboratories, textile and chemical factories produce the wealth that has built Mont-real. All want to be ahead of schedule when summer vacation comes so there's time for hiking and camping, shooting the wild rivers by canoe, fishing and swimming in the province's thousands of lakes. Montrealers head for the hills in summer, and yet the city always has a rear-guard to make sure the café tables don't go empty, and the *cafés-théâtres* put on shows that will appeal to all tastes and interests, with song, poetry, mime, dancing and acting.

Only 150 miles northeast of Montreal stands Quebec City, the political and spiritual capital of the province, which every February unleashes its winter carnival—a madness of lights, music, parades and revelry. Deep down though, Quebec City is sedate and composed, and always returns to the dignified work of governing French Canada; but robust, forward-looking Montreal—with all the excitement of a great metropolis tempered by Gallic *joie-de-vivre*—is something else.

The cruciform Royal Bank building looms over Place Ville-Marie.

A Brief History

Some 22,000 years ago, peoples from Asia came and spread across North America as far as the Atlantic shore. Thousands of years passed, they divided into tribes and clans, and several language groups emerged. But, even by the time of the European discoveries of Canada in the 1500s, these "Indians" were still living a primitive, stone-age life.

The fierce Iroquois inhabited the Quebec region, and had settlements at Stadacona (Quebec City) and Hochelaga (Montreal). They were a sedentary people and lived in "long-houses"—shelters made of bark stretched over a framework of sticks. A number of families might live in one long-house, with only light bark partitions to separate one family's area from another. They grew small crops of grain, corn and wild rice, and kept turkeys for food, but otherwise hunted and fished for what they needed. Pottery, the wheel, iron and intensive agriculture were unknown to them, but they were expert hunters and could track game with an ingenuity now lost to the world. This simple life was to be totally upset by the men in ships who came from across the sea.

The Eskimos

The Eskimos were a later arrival to North America than the Indians, migrating from Asia about 10,000 years ago. They call themselves *Innuit*, which means simply "man." The word "Eskimo" comes from the Algonquin word for "raw flesh eater." The peaceable Eskimos spread to northern regions uninhabited and uncoveted by others. Hunting and fishing—and the daily task of just staying alive in a harsh environment—occupied the Eskimos for thousands of years, but they still found time to craft unique tools (snowshoes, kayaks, dogsleds) and works of art (soapstone figures and prints).

More recently, in moves to safeguard their way of life, the Innuit signed a treaty with the Government of Quebec relating to the land in the area of the giant James Bay hydro-electric power project. But though many of Quebec's growing Eskimo population prefer to live the hardy life of their ancestors, others have settled in towns and villages, often to work in craft or fishing cooperatives—modern forms of organization for their age-old skills.

Innuit carving of woman bundled up for warmth hints at savagery of arctic-like Canadian winter.

Early Explorations

Francis I, king of France (1515–47), was a determined and ambitious ruler. Stirred by the discoveries of Columbus, in 1524 he commissioned Giovanni da Verrazzano to sail across the ocean and explore the New World. Some ten years later, Jacques Cartier, who had been a member of the Verrazzano mission, set out to try and discover a northwest passage round the American continent to the East. He came across a broad, navigable river flowing into the Gulf of St. Lawrence, and was granted the king's permission to explore it. In 1535 he set out to sail up the mighty waterway, stopping at the Indian settlement of Stadacona and finally arriving at Hochelaga, where he was met by over 1,000 curious inhabitants. Seeing the maple-covered hill dominating the village, Cartier christened the place *Mont Réal* (Mount Royal).

Almost 75 years passed be-

fore French interest in the region was fired again and then for a wide variety of mixed motives ranging from economic and political to religious and prestigious: it was, firstly, a rich region with an abundance of raw material; from a strategic point of view, a base here could be a decided advantage in case of war against Spain, helping to cut off Spain's supply of silver from the New World. Furthermore, the avowed—and often genuine—aim of many of the colonists of the time, to spread Christianity, could be carried through. And so, in 1608, a permanent settlement was duly established in Quebec City by Samuel de Champlain. Its success led to others, and in 1642 Paul de Chomedey, Sieur de Maisonneuve, founded the tiny community at Mont Réal and named it Ville-Marie in honor of the Virgin Mary. The vulnerable little party of settlers faced destruction at any moment, for the Iroquois nearby were not friendly. But sustained by their religious faith, they constructed fortifications, a chapel and dwellings.

For a half-century they suffered Iroquois raids, but despite the hostile attacks, the difficult climate and the dangers of the wild forest around them, Ville-Marie grew and prospered. By the early 1700s, the French colonists (around 6,000 of them) were living in peace with the Indians, and the town, now generally called Montreal, was growing rapidly. The trade in furs became more and more profitable, while farming on the rich soil produced bountiful harvests for the people's daily needs.

The English Conquest

The French colonies were not to enjoy peace for long. At the turn of the 17th to 18th centuries, the English and French were engaged in a protracted struggle in Europe and the bitterness extended to the countries' overseas possessions as well. In North America, fighting between the two European powers hardly ever ceased, the fortunes of war favoring first one side then the other. But finally, the issue culminated in a battle which gave the British a decisive victory in Canada.

English forces and colonists from Massachusetts, New York and other American settle-

Maisonneuve, Montreal's founder, is immortalized on Place d'Armes.

14

ments joined in concerted attacks against the French, hoping to capture Quebec. The Indians fought alongside the French to defend the territory against the threat from the south, but the English steadily gained ground. The spearhead of the invasion was aimed at Quebec City, the seat of the French Viceroy. On September 13, 1759, English forces under General James Wolfe reached a grassy and open field near the heights of Quebec City's dramatic promontory, Cap Diamant, and there, on the "Plains of Abraham," engaged the French troops commanded by Louis, Marquis de Montcalm. The fighting was so ferocious that it lasted a bare 30 minutes. At the end, the dead and dying were everywhere, the two generals among them. The French fled into the city, but the English soon overcame all resistance, and the Union Jack was raised over Quebec. Within a year Montreal had fallen as well, and from then on until 1982 the English monarch was Canada's head of state.

In 1775, the rebellious spirit in the American colonies was nearing boiling point. One of the things that had aroused the anger and hostility of the colonists was the passage of the Quebec Act through the Eng-

The Death of General Wolfe *(detail); Benjamin West's classic study from Canada's history.*

lish parliament in 1774. The Act was intended to provide the French Canadians with a more suitable form of government, but the English-speaking colonists of New England interpreted it as being a dangerous and arbitrary concession to Roman Catholicism. A letter, sent by the American Continental Congress to the

king's subjects in Canada, made it clear that in any conflict much of the country would remain loyal to the crown. Thus encouraged, the Continental Army under Richard Montgomery and Benedict Arnold set out to capture Montreal and Quebec City. Though Montreal fell to the American forces, Quebec withstood the siege, and the American bid to take control of Canada was abandoned in 1776.

New People, New Wealth

Commerce in furs kept Montreal rich for almost two centuries, but towards the end of the 1700s, the demand for furs changed, and the city was threatened with economic decline. Soon the Industrial Revolution was affecting much of northern Europe, and the social upheavals were to provide Montreal with a new source of wealth: immigrants. Hoping for a better life in the New World, they brought their skills and their savings using Montreal as a base for settlement. Many went on to fill the vast, fertile farmlands of Ontario and the Canadian prairies to the west, but others stayed and worked to build for the future. By the mid-1800s commerce and industry in the city was booming and the flood of immigration from England, Scotland and Ireland had made it into a predominantly English-speaking city.

With the dawning of the 20th century, the population in Montreal changed again and French-speakers began to outnumber English-speakers, though English remained dominant in business and government. Language became a symbol of a deeper division in society: French-speakers, who were Roman Catholic, were largely excluded from the higher ranks of society by the wealthy, Protestant English-speakers. But Canada was no longer simply a British colony. The Dominion of Canada had been established in 1867 to give Canadians more control over their own affairs, and by the early 1900s Canada was an independent nation in all but name. Still, a tradition of English-speaking dominance continued which French Canadians saw as a threat to their own cultural development. The language question, as a symbol for the deeper problems, became the great challenge to Canada's leaders.

As the British Empire was succeeded by the Commonwealth, the hold of England on her former colonies was weakened even more, and Canadian leaders hoped that this greater autonomy would lead to the solution of the language problem. To signal the country's true state of independence from Britain, the old Canadian flag modeled on the Union Jack was abandoned, and in 1965 the Maple Leaf Flag was adopted.

Firmer Ties to France

Many French Canadians still felt they did not have full opportunity for cultural and economic growth and wanted even greater autonomy: only partition of the country into two language zones, they said, could assure these opportunities. Separatists demonstrated their feelings when Queen Elizabeth and Prince Philip visited Quebec City in 1964: the royal visitors found the streets of the city deserted.

A few years later President de Gaulle of France, while on a state visit to Canada, showed sympathy with the aspirations of French Canadians and exclaimed during a speech, *"Vive le Québec libre!"* ("Long live independent Quebec!''). In late 1976 the Parti Québécois was able to form a government in Quebec and had the chance to begin putting its policies into action. The Quebec National Assembly designated French as the one official language of the province, though the Canadian government recognized both French and English as official languages. Many Quebec officials encourage the move to independence; in 1980, however, the population of Quebec province in a referendum rejected the idea of autonomous statehood.

Montreal's Mouthful
The preservation of French as Quebec's major language is at the heart of Canada's most serious cultural and political problem. Relations between the English- and French-speaking communities have at times been marred by notable struggles, from linguistic harrassment to separatist pressure to terrorism.

The least you can do to get along with the locals is to make an effort—pronouncing a cheerful *bonjour* instead of "good morning" and *merci* for "thanks". If your French peters out after that, no big problem: many French Canadians can, if necessary, speak excellent English. The more so in Montreal, a bilingual city.

As spoken here, French harks back to the 17th century version, but with some picturesque local additions and haphazard borrowing from the Americans. The local lingo is known as *joual,* an approximation of the way they pronounce the French word for horse, *cheval*.

Boom Town
Though the debate over language and heritage goes on, no one disputes that Montrealers, both French and English, have built their city into a major metropolis. The job was not an easy one. After World War I, when Prohibition reigned in the United States, Montreal was "wet," attracting bootleggers and other shady types. The disruption of World War II aggravated the problems of liquor and prostitution until Montreal had a reputation as a city of sin. But in the mid-1950s a reforming mayor, Jean Drapeau, began to "clean up." Besides rooting out corruption and crime, the Drapeau administration forged a new Montreal: slums were replaced with skyscrapers, streets and parks were improved, and the city built one of the best under- **19**

ground transit systems in the world. In 1967 Montreal hosted Expo '67 to show her new face to people from dozens of foreign countries. By the time the 1976 Olympic Games were held in Jean Drapeau's city, Montreal was known as one of the most progressive and exciting cities in the world.

After Maisonneuve's cross on Mount Royal, today the symbol of the new Montreal is the skyscraper built on a cruciform plan which towers above Place Ville-Marie. On its top, a rotary beacon scans the city each night, illuminating what the people of Montreal have accomplished.

RBD Ringier Bilderdienst AG, Zürich

Like latter-day castles, Montreal's skyscrapers "guard" the St. Lawrence.

The St. Lawrence Seaway

Montreal and Quebec City grew up on river commerce carried on by small wooden ships, but with the age of steam and the development of steel boats the cities of the St. Lawrence found that bigger ships were having problems moving up the river; in 1959 this was solved when Queen Elizabeth and President Eisenhower inaugurated the St. Lawrence Seaway *(Voie Maritime du Saint-Laurent)*, a system of locks and canals which made it possible for ocean-going vessels to go from the Atlantic up the St. Lawrence River to the Great Lakes, a distance of almost 2,000 miles. The part next to Ile Sainte-Hélène is the St. Lambert Lock. At the eastern end of the Victoria Bridge, an observatory (charge for admission) allows a good view of the lock's operation and explanatory diagrams guide the visitor through the process.

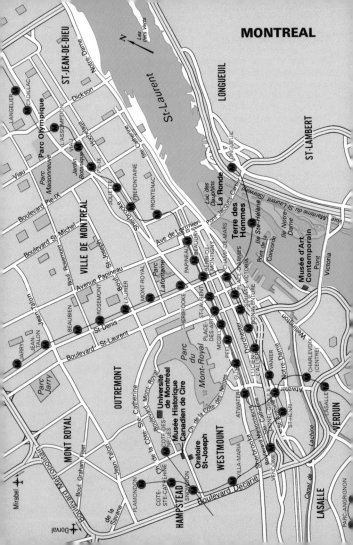

What to See

Just as Maisonneuve climbed Mount Royal to survey his new settlement in 1642, jet-age visitors now do the same to get their bearings. The hill overlooks all Montreal, and from the summit the city's layout is easy to grasp. The great St. Lawrence River flowing from the western Lac des Deux Montagnes passes the city, and then continues its north-easterly journey to the Atlantic. Montreal is on the largest of several islands in the St. Lawrence, a location well suited to commerce, recreation and, in the old times, defense. From the hilltop lookout the low stone buildings of Old Montreal (to the east, near the port) are reminders of the earliest settlement. The city's "spine" is the range of sky-scrapers and striking groups of buildings along Dorchester Boulevard. To the southeast, Victoria Bridge spans the St. Lawrence to connect Montreal Island with the southern shore, while to the left of the bridge two miles down the river Jacques-Cartier Bridge starts from Montreal Island crossing Ile Sainte-Hélène and the Expo '67 site before reaching the southern shore.

Looking north from Mount Royal, the scene is residential and there are many of the city's ethnic neighborhoods. To the southwest, the smaller hill of Westmount can be seen surrounded by huge old houses owned by Montreal's wealthy families. The northwest part of the island is covered with residential and industrial sections stretching all the way across to the neighboring island of Laval.

If the weather is very clear, you can see the low range of the Laurentians to the north. The Green Mountains of Vermont may also be visible if you look in the opposite direction, to the south.

Old Montreal
(Vieux Montréal)

Here's where it all began. Take the Metro to the Champ de Mars station and follow the signs to Old Montreal. Make your way up the hill to the grand **Hôtel de Ville** (City Hall), built in a 19th-century revival of French Renaissance style and finished in 1877. To the west of the Hôtel de Ville is **Place Jacques-Cartier,** starting point for a stroll through the historic heart of the city. The **23**

column in the square is dedicated to Lord Horatio Nelson, the heroic British Admiral of the Battle of Trafalgar, and is the city's oldest monument (1809).

Old Montreal's French heritage springs to life in the quaint stone buildings in and around Place Jacques-Cartier. The French style was well adapted to the rigorous life of the frontier: high, steep-sloping roofs kept snow and ice from accumulating and damaging the structure with their weight; the stone walls and small double-glazed and shuttered windows were sturdy protection against the harshness of the winter weather.

Northeast of Place Jacques-Cartier on Rue Notre-Dame, near the Hôtel de Ville, is the stately **Château de Ramezay,** home of Claude de Ramezay, the French king's viceroy in the city from 1703 to 1724. He had such good taste in houses that this one, which he had built as his residence in 1705, was used by the British when they became masters of Quebec. Later, when the American generals Montgomery and Arnold took the city from the British in 1775 (see p. 17), they appropriated the château as well. Benjamin Franklin stayed here when he was sent by the Continental Congress to cajole Montrealers into supporting the American cause, but he failed; so did the American invasion, and the château was soon again occupied by subjects of the British king. Today Château de Ramezay is a museum displaying souvenirs of the history of Quebec in the 18th century. The building's interior was renovated and modernized as recently as 1977, but the vaults dating from 1705 are original and furnished in the style of a colonial kitchen. The château is open Tuesday through Sunday from 11 a.m. to 4:30 p.m.

At the northwestern corner of Place Jacques-Cartier is the former site of the Silver Dollar Saloon, famed in the early 19th century because of the small fortune—up to 350 U.S. silver dollars—inlaid by the owner in the tavern floor. Practically next door at No. 152 is a tall and thin stone building dating from the end of the 1700s called La Sauvegarde; though renovated at the turn of this

Marigolds in Place Jacques-Cartier offset formality of Hôtel de Ville.

25

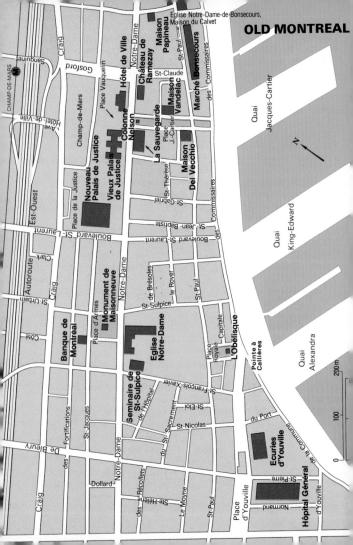

OLD MONTREAL

Église Notre-Dame-de-Bonsecours,
Maison du Calvet

Maison Papineau

Château de Ramezay

Hôtel de Ville

Maison Vandelac

Marché Bonsecours

Colonne Nelson

La Sauvegarde

Maison Del Vecchio

Nouveau Palais de Justice

Vieux Palais de Justice

Banque de Montréal

Monument de Maisonneuve

Église Notre-Dame

L'Obélisque

Pointe à Callières

Séminaire de St-Sulpice

Écuries d'Youville

Hôpital Général

CHAMP-DE-MARS

Quai Jacques-Cartier

Quai King-Edward

Quai Alexandra

200 m

100

0

century, its façade is interesting.

Facing Place Jacques-Cartier are three notable houses, beautifully restored and now used as restaurants. The Vandelac House, to the left of the Hotel Nelson, adds its antique charm to the activities in the square. The Del Vecchio House (1807) is on the square's southern corner, and the Cartier House on the eastern corner.

At the bottom of the square near these houses, turn left onto rue Saint-Paul. The long façade of **Marché Bonsecours** graces the right-hand side of the street. The present building, dating from the middle of the 19th century, was built as a city hall, with offices, a ceremonial hall and market stalls. Now, it accommodates civic departments, including Montreal's housing and planning department.

Past the Marché Bonsecours is the church of **Notre-Dame-de-Bonsecours** (the "Sailors' Church"). In 1657 a chapel was built here for Marguerite Bourgeois, the colony's first schoolteacher, but later destroyed by fire. The present church was finished in 1771, and various modifications and additions have altered its appearance since then. Inside, the wide, low arch of the ceiling is curiously painted in *trompe l'œil* to look like the ceiling of a lofty Gothic cathedral. Very near the port, Notre-Dame-de-Bonsecours was a favorite place of devotion for sailors, who donated model ships they had carved during long sea voyages. These models now hang from the ceiling as symbolic "lamps," fitted with tiny electric bulbs. In the morning on a bright day, the church is especially pretty as sunlight streams through the stained glass windows on the south wall. A small museum here features dioramas depicting the life and work of Marguerite Bourgeois in Old Montreal; the church tower is open to visitors, and offers a sweeping view of Old Montreal and the harbor.

Old Montreal is filled with history: the best way to enter the world of the past is to explore a house of the past. The **Calvet House** (1725), across rue Saint-Paul from Notre-Dame-de-Bonsecours church, has been restored and fitted with pieces from the Montreal Museum of Fine Arts' collection of antique Quebec furniture. Wide, rough-hewn floorboards and casement windows to keep out the icy winter air contrast strangely with elegant furniture. Period paintings, a small hooked rug, lanterns, clocks and china complete the picture of upper-class life in the early French colony.

The wooden beams above the top-floor bedroom of the house show how the roofs were designed to withstand the blizzards of a Montreal winter. Take a look at the framed copy of *The Quebec Gazette* on the ground floor, dating from 1786 and printed in both English and French—an early effort at bilingualism!

Southwest of Place Jacques-Cartier, six blocks along rue Notre-Dame, is the **Place d'Armes,** with its monument to Montreal's founder, Maisonneuve. **Notre-Dame Church** on the square, a center of Roman Catholic worship in the city, is a must for any visitor to Montreal. Designed by an Irishman, James O'Donnell, the opulence of the interior, redecorated by Victor Bourgeau in the 1870s, appeals to the Quebecer's love of French tradition, while the lavish use of native carved wood figures and designs makes the church familiar and uniquely Québécois. Built in 1829, though not completed until the 1840s, Notre-Dame is not the city's oldest church, but it is certainly the most beloved.

The great bell is one of the

Marguerite Bourgeois
In 1653, Marguerite Bourgeois decided to devote her life to educating the youth of the growing colony in Montreal and said good-bye forever to her native town of Troyes, in Champagne. Sailing for New France with the encouragement of Maisonneuve, she came with three marriageable girls "of good character" to teach in her school and establish wholesome households in the colony. The experiment worked, and later she encouraged other young women to come to Montreal. With this enterprising public relations effort, early Montreal took on some of the refinements of civilization, softening the harsh frontier-town atmosphere. Marguerite Bourgeois and her followers later formed an order of nuns, the Congregation of Notre-Dame, to continue teaching in the colony. Three hundred years after she landed in Montreal, Marguerite Bourgeois was officially canonized a saint.

1725 Calvet House is a treasure-chest of old Quebec. Exhibits include the Quebec Gazette, *sign of the province's early bilingualism.*

THE QUEBEC GAZETTE.

LA GAZETTE DE QUEBEC.

NUMB. 1069.

THURSDAY, FEBRUARY 9, 1786.

JEUDI, le 9 FEVRIER, 1786.

CONSTANTINOPLE, September 30.

THE Bashaw of Scutari has transmitted to the Divan the history of his expedition against the Montenegrins, and has accounted for the hostilities committed on the Venetian territory; by alledging, that they were become necessary, on account of the refusal made for the Ottoman troops of the passage through the territory of Venice.

Berlin, October 14. The King, our Sovereign, lies dangerously ill of his old hereditary disorder, which has, however, attacked him at this time with uncommon fury, so as to alarm his physicians, he, himself, however, retains the utmost serenity and firmness. Neither the Prince or his Royal uncle are yet returned from the review at Magdeburg Marche, which we hear is over, and was uncommonly magnificent. The number of nobility, &c. is reported to have been numerous, past all former comparison.

Hague, October 19. The residence of the Stadtholderian family of his old hereditary disorder, which has, meaning to be, not to return to the Hague until justice shall be done him (which may possibly keep him away all the winter) makes a dangerous sensation here. The people of the Hague are not very tender when they are hungry now, will be the case this winter, by the privation of 100,000 florins, given annually by the Stadtholderian family, shall put the poor of the hinger, and perhaps make them rise in favour of a Prince, whom some persons strive in vain to render odious to them. These considerations do actually cause some

CONSTANTINOPLE, 30 Septembre.

LE Bacha de Scutari a transmis au Divan l'histoire de son expédition contre les Montenegrins, et a rendu compte des hostilités commises sur les territoires Venitiens; alléguant qu'elles étoient devenues nécessaires, à cause du refus que l'on avoit fait de livrer passage aux troupes Ottomanes sur les terres de Venise.

Berlin, 14 Octobre. Le Roi notre souverain est dangereusement malade de son ancienne maladie héréditaire, qui pour cette fois l'a attaqué avec une violence extraordinaire, de façon que les médecins en ont été alarmés. Il conserve cependant toute la tranquilité et fermeté possible. Le Prince ni son oncle Royal ne sont pas encore retournés de la revue de Magdebourg March, qui, à ce que nous apprenons, est finie, et a été extraordinairement magnifique. On rapporte que le nombre de noblesse, &c. y a été plus grand que l'on ait encore vû.

La Haie, 19 Octobre. La résidence de la famille du Stadthouder en Friesland, et la résolution du Prince, qui semble être de ne point retourner à la Haie, qu'on ne lui ait rendu justice (ce qui pourra peut-être le retenir absent tout l'hiver) fait ici une dangereuse sensation. Le peuple de la Haie n'est pas fort tendre lorsqu'il a faim; or qu'arrivera-t-il ce hiver lorsque la privation de cent mille florins données annuellement par la famille Stadthoudérienne mettra les pauvres hors d'état de subsister, et les fera peut-être soulever en faveur d'un Prince, que quelques personnes s'efforcent en vain de lui rendre odieux. Ces considérations causent actuellement de l'inqui-

largest on earth; called Le Gros Bourdon, it weighs 12 tons.

Annexed to the main church, a simpler but still impressive **Chapel of the Sacred Heart** is located behind the main altar. The chapel was destroyed by fire in 1978, but has been reconstructed. The decoration of the vast ceiling, that was previously quite a feature, has been redone partially as before, partially in a contemporary style. Also behind the main altar, next to the chapel, is a small museum devoted to souvenirs and memorabilia of Roman Catholicism in Montreal. Besides other items displayed are two fascinating **paintings** by Pierre-Adolphe-Arthur Guindon (1864–1923). Guindon, a Sulpician monk interested in the Iroquois culture, was an accomplished painter and his pictures of *The Singing Monster* and *The Spirit of the Lac des Deux Montagnes* approach surrealism. Another treasure in the museum's collection is a gorgeous antependium embroidered by Jeanne Le Ber (1695–1724) in gold, silver and brightly colored threads.

Inside Notre Dame church—fitting testimonial to its architect, who was converted while building it.

Beside Notre-Dame Church in the Place d'Armes is the group of stone buildings (said to be the oldest in Montreal) housing the Seminary of Saint-Sulpice. The curious clock on the façade (1710) was driven by a wooden movement until the turn of the century.

Facing the church from across the Place d'Armes, the domed building is the **Bank of Montreal.** The city's oldest, it's an impressive structure of marble, granite and brass. In the entrance hall, shiny black pillars frame a statue of *Patria* dedicated to the "Men Who Fell in the Great War, 1914–1918." The grand hall of the Exchange Room, behind the statue, is worth a look because of its size and very substantial furnishings. Off the entrance hall is a small banking museum featuring a teller's window modeled on that of the first bank (1817) and various other mementos.

Named after the lady who founded Montreal's order of Les Sœurs Grises (The Gray Nuns), Place d'Youville is very near the spot where tradition has it Maisonneuve built the little fort he called Ville-Marie. A fanciful little brick building which was Montreal's old fire station stands in the middle of the square's parking area, and

next to the fire station is the entrance to the **Youville Stables** (*Ecuries d'Youville*). The gray stone buildings, identified by the bull's-eye windows under the eaves, enclose a fine courtyard very much in keeping with the spirit of Old Montreal, even though the buildings only date from the early 1800s. They were not really designed as stables (nearby wooden structures, gone now, served that purpose), but rather as factories, warehouses and offices;

one section was used by the Gray Nuns as a hospital. Restoration by a group of Montreal businessmen has made the Youville Stables one of the most attractive addresses in town, and several firms have rented office space there. In summer, part of the courtyard serves as an outdoor restaurant and open-air theater.

Walk northeast through the square from the Youville Stables and look down the Rue du Port on the right, for a view of

Fashionable addresses in Montreal: Youville Stables (left) and Habitat.

the architecturally advanced dwelling complex called **Habitat,** a collection of modular living spaces, breezeways and outdoor areas which gives the impression of a veritable "airborne village"—a modern castle in the air.

At the eastern corner of the Place d'Youville, where the square meets the Rue de la Commune, is a spot called Pointe-à-Callières, once a point of land extending out into the water at the end of which was Maisonneuve's first fort. Across the street in the small Place Royale you'll find an obelisk commemorating the founding of the city in 1642.

33

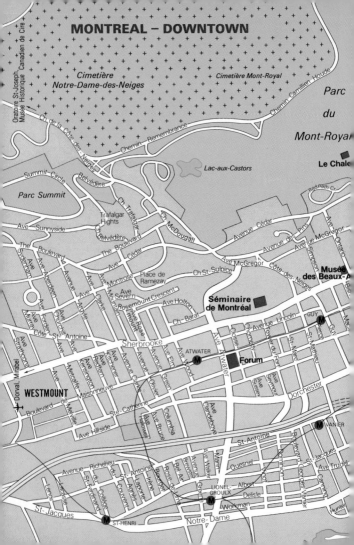

MONTREAL – DOWNTOWN

Cimetière
Notre-Dame-des-Neiges

Cimetière Mont-Royal

Oratoire St-Joseph
Musée Historique Canadien de Cre

Parc
du
Mont-Royal

Chemin – Remembrance

Chemin Camillien Houde

Lac-aux-Castors

Le Chale

Ch de la Côte-des-Neiges

Summit Circle

Belvédère

Redpath Cr

Parc Summit

Trafalgar
Hights

Ch Trafalgar

Ch McDougall

Ave Sunnyside

Belvédère

The Boulevard

Avenue – Cédar

Avenue des Pins

Avenue McGregor

Avenue Cédar

Ave McGregor

Ave Ontario

Ave Cédar

Côte-des-Neiges

Musée
des Beaux-A

Montrose

Place de
Ramezay

Ch St-Sulpice

The
Sydenham

Ave
Aberdeen

Ave
Forden

Avenue – Argyle

Ch Clarke

Ave
Clarke

Ave Severn

Rosemount Crescent

Ave Holton

Séminaire
de Montréal

Ave
Murray

Côte St-Antoine

Mont Rose

Ch Barat

Avenue Lincoln

Boulevard du Parc

Rue Simpson

Guy

M

Ma

Sherbrooke

Ave Elm

Ave Wood

ATWATER

M

Ave Atwater

Ave du Musée

Ave St-Marc

Avenue Lincoln

St-Mathieu

Guy

Strathcona

Ave
Kitchener

Avenue – Redfern

Avenue – Olivier

Green

Forum

Ave
Seymour

Dorval, Mirabel

Ave
Metcalfe

Ave
Melville

Maisonneuve

Ste-Catherine

Ave Elm

Ave Columbia

Ave Clandeboye

Dorchester

WESTMOUNT

Boulevard

Ave Hillside

Ave
Halliwell

Ave Ethel

M VANIER

St-Antoine

Boulevard Georges-Vanier

St-Jacques

Ave Trudel

Avenue – Richelieu

Avenue
St-Antoine

Rue Irène

Laporte

Ave
Brewster

Rose Art

Ave Walker

Quesnel

Domenion

Albert

Ave Cazelais

Delisle

Canning

Hunter

Au
Couvent

Laprés

LIONEL
GROULX

St-Ferdinand

St-Jacques

M ST-HENRI

Notre-Dame

Workman

A Walk Downtown

Near the foot of Mount Royal, downtown Montreal hums with activity. Certain landmarks tower above the urban jumble: the cruciform office tower of the Place Ville-Marie, Montreal's earliest effort at urban renewal and the stylish Château Champlain hotel, which is described as either "wedding cake" or "kitchen grater," depending on one's taste. The Canadian Imperial Bank of Commerce, yet another skyscraper, has a proper observatory at the top.

The axis of the city's downtown area, Boulevard René-Lévesque bisects **Dominion Square,** starting-place for explorations of Montreal's heart by foot. Coach tours also leave from here. Or hire a horse-drawn *calèche* (carriage); they wait on Dominion Square.

In warm weather this plot of greenery is an open-air art gallery, splashed with the canvases

of young Canadian painters displayed for the passer-by or prospective buyer. The bright colors of the paintings and of the flower-vendors' wagons contrast with the dark tones of the square's sober statues to Robert Burns, early Canadian prime ministers Laurier and MacDonald, and to Canadian soldiers who fell in the Boer War; but Henry Moore's *Reclining Nude* lends a lighter touch.

Today the square is surrounded by towering commercial palaces: the Sun Life Building, Dominion Square Building, and the Canadian Imperial Bank.

Artists, fountains, bring a hint of Paris to this second-largest French-speaking city in the world.

Walk northeast along the boulevard and you pass in front of the Roman Catholic cathedral of Montreal, named **Marie-Reine-du-Monde.** Dedicated in 1870, it's an authentic copy, though half the size, of St. Peter's in Rome.

Just past the church is one of Montreal's outstanding hotels, the Queen Elizabeth *(Le Reine Elizabeth),* which towers yet higher above the Central Station *(Gare Centrale).* Across from the hotel's main entrance is **Place Ville-Marie,** a complex of modern office buildings of which the most impressive is the Royal Bank's cross-shaped tower, designed by I. M. Pei. The Quebec Government maintains a Tourist Information Office at the northern corner of Place Ville-Marie, near the intersection of Cathcart and University Streets.

Go northwest along University Street to St. Catherine Street and **Christ Church Cathedral.** This very authentic-looking English Gothic church would have made Chaucer feel at home, though in fact it was built just a century ago; it's the seat of the Bishop of Montreal.

St. Catherine is Montreal's main shopping thoroughfare; crowds flock up and down it winter and summer alike with those out to buy or just to look. Walking southwest along the street from Christ Church Cathedral you'll pass the city's large, established department stores and many smaller shops. Movie theaters, travel agencies, delicatessens and cafeterias, plus a few boutiques and bars, all add to the color and variety.

Nine blocks west from Christ Church along St. Catherine is the intersection with **Crescent Street** which, with neighboring Mountain and Bishop Streets, is one of the centers of Montreal's boutique and bistro areas. A dozen city blocks were saved from the upheaval of urban renewal, and the Victorian stone row-houses have been preserved, refurbished, painted brightly, and converted into exclusive or off-beat shops, chic bars and restaurants.

Walk up Crescent to **Sherbrooke Street,** another major thoroughfare. Here, you find yourself in the middle of Sherbrooke's antique shop section. Mingled with the elegant antique shops are others display-

Montreal cathedral—a haven for the spirit in a sea of commerce.

ing costly goods such as oriental carpets, silver and furs. Very near the intersection of Crescent and Sherbrooke is Montreal's **Museum of Fine Arts** *(Musée des Beaux Arts)*, a popular place for spending a few hours (see p. 72).

Continuing on a zigzag course through downtown, walk northeast on Sherbrooke for six blocks to reach the main gates of McGill University, one of Montreal's four great universities (McGill and Concordia are anglophone, the Université de Montréal and the Université du Québec à Montréal are francophone). Though chartered by the king in 1821, McGill did not really begin to take its present shape until the 1860s. Its founder, a Scot named James McGill, had come to Canada to make his fortune in the fur trade; though he never saw the university's opening, the funds and land were his bequest to the city. Widely acclaimed as an institution with high standards, student enrolment today is near 15,000.

Roll back the years on a sleigh ride through Mount Royal Park.

Mount Royal Park
(Parc du Mont-Royal)

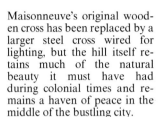

Maisonneuve's original wooden cross has been replaced by a larger steel cross wired for lighting, but the hill itself retains much of the natural beauty it must have had during colonial times and remains a haven of peace in the middle of the bustling city.

A footpath and stairs, open summer and winter, lead from the end of Peel Street through the park to the summit of Mount Royal. Good for a more gradual climb on foot or by car, "Remembrance Road" on the northwest side of the park, winds up the hillside as well.

Funded by the city, Mount Royal Park was designed by Frederick Law Olmstead, who also planned New York's Central Park and Boston's Fenway Park. Since the late 19th century its roads, paths, picnic areas, lookouts, a pond and other facilities have made it one of Montreal's favorite green spaces. **Beaver Lake** *(Lac des Castors)*, halfway up the hillside, is the place for ice skating and sledding in winter, for quiet strolls along the shore or picnics in summer. Just slightly farther up towards the summit from the lake is an outdoor **41**

Montrealers relax in the leafy shade of Mount Royal Park.

sculpture display, next to the **Mount Royal Art Centre** *(Centre d'Art du Mont-Royal),* which features exhibitions winter and summer. And at the top of the hill, the terrace of the Chalet Lookout offers a **panoramic view** of the city. The Chalet itself is a rather grand stone and Nordic-timbered hall bedecked with the flags of many nations inside. The carved wooden squirrels which are part of the interior archwork seem almost as real as the

tame ones which eat tidbits from your hand as you sit admiring the view on the benches outside.

There are many ways to explore Mount Royal Park, including the *calèche* (carriage); drivers will gladly take you from Dominion Square to the top of the hill and down again.

In winter snow, the drivers harness their horses to sleighs and wait near Beaver Lake. Or try jogging up the hill, like the more athletic Montrealers, in all seasons. Winter also brings out the cross-country skiiers and snowshoe owners who use the well-marked trails winding through the park. **43**

Montreal's "Complexes"

(Metro: Place des Arts)

Montreal's Place des Arts was planned and started in the 1950's, though the concert hall, **Salle Wilfrid-Pelletier,** didn't open until 1963. Contemporary in design, the façade of the concert hall nevertheless follows harmonious classic lines. Tapestries and sculptures by Canadian artists decorate the foyer, including a soapstone sculpture by the Eskimo artist Innukpuk.

A center of cultural activities, something is always happening on the Place des Arts. A monthly calendar of events is issued free and is available in tourist offices and hotels.

City within a city, the multi-million dollar Complexe Desjardins is certainly one of Montreal's most exciting examples of modern architecture.

Before some performances a snack can be had in the foyer of the Salle Wilfrid-Pelletier at lunchtime; reserve your place and your tickets in advance.

As part of the Place des Arts, the **Complexe Desjardins** is one of the city's most exciting examples of modern architecture—an under-and-over complex built by La Haye-Ouellet and Blouin in 1976 (across Sainte-Catherine from the concert hall). Enter the grand glass portals on Sainte-Catherine and you find a self-contained multi-level environment of terraces, balconies, mezzanines and a sunken plaza covering a full acre. Light and airy, with small waterfalls, fountains, trees and garden plots, the central area provides a perfectly harmonious environment.

Design is based on several geometric shapes appearing frequently in crystalline patterns, both in the grand conception of the buildings and in details of decor. Colors reflect Montreal's cityscape, with Montreal's favorite silvery-gray predominating, set off here and there by flashes of bright color. Texture is also handled very successfully—the concrete, metal and glass of the modern city softened by benches and railings of natural wood. Perhaps the happiest triumph in the design is that the complex is no sterile showpiece and is used by everyone—from shoppers and out-of-town visitors, to workers in the adjoining business and government office buildings, who come to the plaza for lunch or a coffee-break. Finally, a statistic: this complex cost its sponsors—the private consortium and the Quebec government—around $100 million.

From the Complexe Desjardins, you can walk underground to the **Complexe Guy-Favreau.** Formerly the site of Montreal's Chinatown, this complex comprises the federal government administrative services, commercial space, conference centers and apartments. Happily, the Chinese Catholic Mission church and adjoining school have been renovated and incorporated into this vast ensemble.

Continuing south, you'll see a gigantic green typewriter, which is in fact the **Palais des Congrès.** The whole façade is an enormous glass wall which illuminates the entrance hall and access to the circulation areas. This building can accommodate up to 5,800 people in 31 conference rooms; the kitchen is equipped to serve gourmet banquets for 4,800 guests!

The City Underground

They say it all began by accident, when someone suggested that there should be a few shops under the Place Ville-Marie complex which was being built. The idea was blown up into an urban underground connecting major centers by walkways, themselves joined to Metro stations, so that during the long, cold, wet winter one could work, shop, go to a movie or have dinner without having to brave the elements. It's quite a curious feeling to walk out of your hotel in bad weather without overcoat, raincoat or boots for a night on the town!

Start your wanderings through the city underground where it began—on Place Ville-Marie. Occupying part of the complex are the Queen Elizabeth Hotel and the Central Station, along with a Quebec Liquor Corporation (Société des Alcools) store, many elegant shops, several restaurants, discothèques and taverns. There is no Metro station on Place Ville-Marie, but you can get to one without going outside. Follow the signs to the Central Station, walk through the station hall and then continue to Place Bonaventure. Take the escalator down to Le Passage, a subterranean passageway to Place Bonaventure.

The **Place Bonaventure** complex is a major part of the city underground. Montreal's main exhibition hall is located here, along with a Metro station and an international shopping center called Le Viaduc, where each shop carries products from a different foreign country. The Hotel Bonaventure is a favorite with convention groups, perhaps because of its attractive roof-top swimming pool. In a tiny court furnished with trees and benches, the pool is surrounded by the hotel building but is open to the sky all year round. In winter the poolside is covered by wind-sculptured snowdrifts and the pool is heated and brightly lit from underwater. Steam rises in great clouds as swimmers luxuriate in the warmth of the water. A tunnel connecting the outdoor pool in the court with an interior one next to the changing rooms allows swimmers to glide from indoors to outdoors without ever leaving the water.

Other entertainment on Place Bonaventure includes two movie theaters and several restaurants, plus a nightclub.

Follow the Metro signs to the Bonaventure station, and then (without entering the Metro) to

Windsor Station (1886), designed by Bruce Price, the architect responsible for the famous Château-Frontenac in Quebec City. Usually a delightful panoramic showing of works by Canadian painters will be set up in a little impromptu gallery on the main concourse. Walk back toward the Bonaventure Metro and then follow signs to the Place du Canada, site of the impressive **Château Champlain Hotel,** with its movie house, disco,

Montreal's Metro is the city's pride: efficient, clean, quiet and attractive.

supper club and cocktail lounge.

In another corner of the city underground, **Les Terrasses,** off St. Catherine Street, is near the McGill Metro station. A bit like the Complexe Desjardins, several trees decorate the central open space of this area, with the "terraces" rising from sub-ground level. **47**

St. Helen's Island
(Ile Sainte-Hélène)
(Metro: Ile Sainte-Hélène)

One of the city's most popular summer attractions is on the Ile Sainte-Hélène in the St. Lawrence. After its very successful year as Expo '67, the site of Montreal's world fair be-

Riding high: novel attractions at La Ronde, Montreal's amazing amusement park, thrill the clients.

came a permanent exhibition ground with the name **Man and His World** *(Terre des Hommes).*  The fun and adventure of a world's fair are found here every day of the week during the summer: national pavilions (charge for admission), outdoor concerts, exhibits and films on the subjects of ecology, urban life and Canadian history are all open for a visit. The architecture is futuristic, the atmosphere that of a very attractive amusement park.

La Ronde, one of the world's best amusement parks, is part of Man and His World. It is often compared to Copenhagen's famous Tivoli Gardens because of its myriad entertainments and its bright, happy-go-lucky feeling. You can choose from among dozens of different rides, including the exquisite torture of a whirligig called the Gyrotron. A model French Canadian Village gives visitors a glimpse into Quebec's past and the outdoor beer garden is a life-saver on a hot summer afternoon. The park is open only during the summer, beginning on weekends only in May and the first half of June;

from mid-June until September it's open every day. You can enter the park anytime after 1 p.m. and stay until past midnight.

While visiting Ile Sainte-Hélène stop in to see the Military and Maritime Museum in the **Old Fort** *(Le Vieux Fort)*. Besides the weapons and displays in the museum's collection, military units stage fancy marching parades and precision drill—a colorful show for all the family.

Botanical Gardens
(Jardin Botanique)
(Metro: Pie IX)

A few quiet hours in the 200-acre grounds of the Botanical Gardens are a refreshing change from Montreal's exciting pace. In warm weather

Alongside Botanical Gardens is prestigious 1976 Olympic stadium.

all the gardens' 20,000 different species and varieties of plants are on display in formal and informal plots laced with walkways and the tracks of a miniature sightseeing train. Plants are identified by the Latin or scientific name and the English and/or French common names where applicable.

The park, started in 1931 by Brother Marie-Victorin, a local botanist, is open every day of the week throughout the year with no charge for admission.

Cacti, tropical plants and others requiring special environments are nurtured in glass conservatories, which can be seen even when snow covers the acres of outdoor gardens. The variety is stunning and the plants are tended with real devotion.

Olympic Stadium in Maisonneuve Park next to the Gardens, was the site of the 1976 games; the mammoth stadium can seat over 70,000 people and the swimming complex boasts

Jean Drapeau

In 1954 a report was issued by Judge Caron of Montreal, who had been looking into corruption and moral decline in the city. The Caron report was a bombshell; in effect, it said that no Montrealer could be proud of such a city. Only three weeks after the report was released, one of Judge Caron's chief investigators, 38-year-old Jean Drapeau, was elected Mayor of Montreal on a reform ticket. Three years later, he lost the seat to a rival candidate, but in 1960 the electorate decided that Drapeau was indeed the better man, and he was swept into power again and served as mayor for many years. Though some of his bold plans were highly controversial, most Montrealers credit him with being the founder of the "new Montreal."

half a dozen pools. Each has a different purpose, from the regulation Olympic-size racing pool to a scuba pool 50 feet deep. One of the most popular and frequently-visited facilities is the Vélodrome, complete with a redwood track for the bicycle races so loved by anyone linked to France. Boxing, wrestling and basketball matches are also held here in the central space. Guided tours of the Olympic Stadium are offered daily.

The bold conception of the Olympic facilities is typical of Montreal, but it caused problems as well. The city, the province and all Canada were enthusiastic and attentive hosts for the games, but the costs of construction and the apportioning of the expense remained hotly debated topics for some time after the games when it was decided the citizens of Montreal would pay the bill.

St. Joseph's Oratory
(Oratoire Saint-Joseph)
(Metro: Snowdon or Côte-des-Neiges)

From the city's high points, the huge dome of St. Joseph's Oratory floats on the skyline in Westmount. Brother André, a humble monk of the Holy Cross order, found that he had miraculous powers for curing people who came to him for help, a service he performed faithfully until his death in 1904. St. Joseph was the healer of the sick and Brother André's dream was to have a place of worship erected to the saint's glory, a wish that eventually came true. Brother André's tomb was already a place of pilgrimage for the sick, and the magnificent oratory became an even stronger inducement to come to this "Canadian Lourdes." Services in the chapel (1904), the crypt-church (1916) and the modern basilica (completed in 1960) are usually held in French.

Brother André's tomb and a votive chapel with the crypt-church, are on the entry level. Elsewhere in the oratory you'll see replicas of the rooms in which Brother André lived, worked and died, photographs and memorabilia of him, a 15-minute film on his life and work, a museum, and the impressive basilica. Though built on the classic plan, the basilica is very modern in design and decoration. Its lofty, spacious nave is free of cumbersome detail, and only the dramatic, important features such as the altar and the windows are emphasized.

Up the hillside behind the oratory winds a path to the stations of the cross in a lovely garden setting.

Montreal's Neighborhoods

Urban redevelopment has given Montreal many impressive landmarks but the city holds far more than just big buildings and grand design. Many residential sections on the old-fashioned human scale are alive with daily neighborhood activity.

To find diverting local color, go to **Square Saint-Louis** via Rue Saint-Denis going west from the Berri-de-Montigny Metro station. Saint-Denis is a lively university street, lined with student cafés, sandwich shops, boarding houses and small bistros. Several blocks up the hill is Square Saint-Louis (Metro *Sherbrooke*), a picturesque area of Victorian gingerbread houses, contrasting amusingly with murals on the blank walls of buildings, and denizens dressed à la Greenwich Village. The charm of the square is diminished somewhat by the huge State Tourism School at the northeast end.

The southwest end of the square is connected to Boulevard Saint-Laurent (St. Lawrence)—a big shopping district —by **Rue Prince Arthur,** a fine pedestrian way paved in tiles,

lined with shady trees, and filled with strollers in the evening. It also offers murals, little shops and restaurants featuring exotic specialties. **Boulevard Saint-Laurent** itself is full of ethnic shops. The grocery stores carry foods from all over the world. Restaurants serve Japanese, Polish, Middle Eastern and especially Italian and Spanish dishes. All this diversity produces its own amusements: shop signs are sometimes misspelled in *both* of Montreal's major languages as immigrants to this bilingual city find themselves struggling with two unfamiliar tongues.

In fact the whole area between Boulevard Saint-Laurent and Parc Lafontaine north to Avenue du Mont-Royal has recently been undergoing a tremendous upheaval and change. Lots of small houses have been taken over and done up to become chic boutiques, exotic clothes shops, groceries, cafés, restaurants, *cafés-théâtres,* and so on.

If the Saint-Laurent is Montreal's "Little Europe", the Orient is ever-present on six blocks delimited by Dorchester and Viger north and south, and by Sainte-Dominique and Saint-Urbain east and west (Metro: *Place d'Armes*). Here you'll catch whiffs of spicy odors from Chinese restaurants and grocery stores. The Sino-Canadian community remain close-knit and courageous in the face of urban renewal officials who covet this area on the edge of the financial district, and who have already taken over a large part of Chinatown for their Palais des Congrès and Guy-Favreau complex.

Rue Prince Arthur and denizens reveal an artistic vocation.

Excursions

Into the Laurentians
(Les Laurentides)

The gracious rolling mountains, an hour's drive north of Montreal, were first inhabited by Algonquin Indians looking for a safe place away from their enemies, the Iroquois. They may also have chosen the region for its natural beauty. Long, narrow glacial lakes are fed by cold streams bubbling down the mountains' wooded slopes of yellow birch, beech, pine and maple. The small towns here make their living partly through the resort business, providing accommodation, restaurants both plain and fancy, hunting and fishing supplies and the necessary equipment for the many sports here. The wild beauty of the Laurentians is preserved intact in the very large provincial parks and reservations of which the most famous and popular is **Mont Tremblant.**

From Montreal you can easily reach the Laurentians by hourly Voyageur bus service (Metro: *Berri-de-Montigny*) or private car. Highway 15, the Autoroute of the Laurentians (a toll road), is direct and passes near many small towns. Highway 117 takes up the route where 15 ends to bring vacationers within easy reach of access to the parks.

Several towns in the region have monuments to Curé Labelle, after whom one of the Laurentian forest reservations is named, for he is the man who did the most to settle the region. During the latter part of the 19th century, when Quebecers were being drawn to New England textile mills by steady work and good pay, Labelle encouraged people to move and farm the Laurentian region. He explored much of the territory on foot and personally founded many Laurentian towns. Today farming, tourism and some industry (principally logging and papermaking) keep the mountain area prosperous without detracting from its natural beauty.

During the warm summer months, visitors enjoy many outdoor sports, especially lake activities such as boating, sailing, water-skiing, swimming and fishing for speckled and lake trout, pike, bass, walleye, the "fighting muskellunge" and other varieties of fresh-water fish. Canoe or kayak trips, with camping out along the riverbank, are one of the best ways

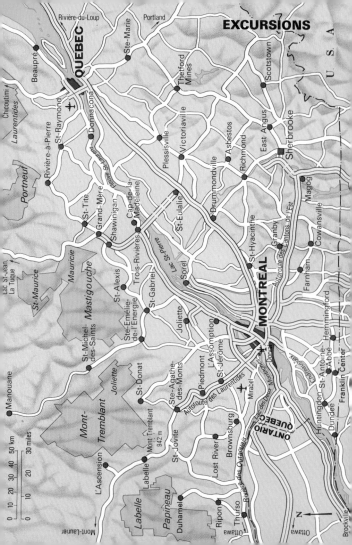

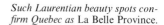
Such Laurentian beauty spots confirm Quebec as La Belle Province.

to appreciate the rugged splendor of the mountains. Hiking is another, and is especially good in the provincial parks, or, for the less active, picnic sites abound throughout the region.

In winter the Laurentian colors change from green and blue to white and gray, bringing crowds of skiers to the ski runs on almost every hillside north of the town of Piedmont (40 miles north of Montreal) all the way to Mont Tremblant Park. The slopes of Mont Tremblant descend over 2,000 feet from summit to base, and are laced with some 65 miles of downhill trails served by chairlifts and T-bars. It seems as though each of the large resort hotels (and even some of the more modest places) has its own mountain, lifts, ski-school and special attractions in the way of cuisine and après-ski entertainment. Cross-country skiing *(ski de fond)* is also popular. Most people who come to the Laurentians for skiing sign up for a "package" *(forfait)* including accommodation, meals **59** and lift fees for a weekend or a full week. Proud owners of a new pair of Eskimo-made snowshoes can try them out on the 6 miles of snowshoe trails in Mont Tremblant Park, or at other centers.

Springtime brings "sugaring-off" (see box) in the groves of sugar maple trees; and in autumn it may be too chilly for a picnic, but just right for a drive to see the brilliant fall foliage.

The Sugar Maple

The maple tree is Canada's chief symbol, with the famed red maple leaf the emblem of her flag. In the early springtime, usually about March, when the weather brings cold nights and bright warmish days, Quebecers head out to the sugar bushes (that is, groves of sugar maples) to put buckets under the little tapping pipes which have been driven into the maple trunks. When the sap is running at its peak, this process can result in a bucketful from each tree by evening. The sap is then taken to the sugar house, a structure housing large vats heated by wood fires. There it is boiled down for several days, until each 40 gallons of liquid is reduced to one gallon of light golden maple syrup with a very hearty flavor.

When packed in sterilized containers, maple syrup will last for many months and when crystallized it makes maple sugar candy. A touch of maple syrup added to *fèves au lard* is essential if the dish is to be authentic, and maple sugar pie is yet another not to be missed Quebec delicacy.

"Sugaring off," the pouring of the hot thickened sap of the sugar maple onto the snow is fun for all the family and shouldn't be missed if you're in Montreal during the sugaring-off season in spring. Newspapers carry advertisements from local farmers who welcome visitors; or contact the tourist information office.

The Cider Road
(Chemin du Cidre)

If you have a car or rent one for a day, the autumn apple-picking season is a good excuse for a trip to the towns south and east of Montreal. Before you leave the city, check with the Quebec Tourism Office in Place Ville-Marie for news of current festivals, cider-making celebrations and special events. The "Cider Road" described here is a favorite Montreal outing.

Due south of Montreal is Huntingdon County, reached by Autoroute 15. Drive west along Highway 202, near the New York border, to the small town of Hemmingford. In mid-August the town holds its annual apple festival, when the orchards are full of heavily-laden trees and the cider houses give free tours. Handicrafts, antiques and "precious junk" are on sale at sidewalk booths, and the atmosphere is heady, healthy and happy. The festival is in anticipation of the harvest season rather than in celebration of harvest, for the fruit in the orchards is only ready for picking in September and October.

If you're around Hemmingford in late September or early October, be sure to go to the Saint-Bernard cider cellars just outside town for a tour and a demonstration of cider-making, plus a sampling of the "wine of Quebec." The cellars are open weekdays only, and reservations are not necessary here, though they are required at many other cider houses. Hemmingford is also noted for its African Safari Park, a 400-acre reserve harboring lions, elephants, rhinos and lots of other exotic creatures (open summer only).

Franklin Center, farther along Highway 202, is the home of the Quebec Apple-Growers' Association *(Coopérative des Pomiculteurs du Québec)*, and their cider plant is open by appointment to visitors who would like to sample their wares. Another cider house—Saint-Antoine-Abbé—is also open by appointment on weekday afternoons and evenings. You might also stop by to see Blair House, a historic old farm which has been restored and converted into the historical museum of the Chateauguay Valley.

Home-made maple-sugar candy is a rapturous rediscovery each spring.

🕴 A Day in Quebec City

Quebec was the first French city in Canada, and is today the capital of the province of Quebec and the home of the Quebec parliament, called the National Assembly. French influence is clearly predominant here, and the English aspect is much less obvious than in Montreal. In Quebec City, you will find your French dictionary and phrase book invaluable.

The city's history matches its dramatic situation on Cap Diamant, an outcrop of rock commanding the St. Lawrence. The explorer-trapper Samuel de Champlain founded the town in 1608, building a small fortified *Abitation* (dwelling) near a good docking place on the shore, but soon moved to a more easily-defensible cliff-top site near where the Château-Frontenac stands today. Over the years the town expanded as the fur-trade increased, and as it grew it developed culturally as well. A Jesuit seminary was founded in 1663 and two centuries later this school became Laval University.

In 1759 the English sent a crack force of British marines and regulars who laid siege to the town and after almost three months of a standoff, the British general, James Wolfe, succeeded in getting his soldiers onto the heights at the southern approach to the Upper Town. He was met by the Marquis de Montcalm and his troops. On the field now called the "Plains of Abraham", fierce fighting raged for less than a half-hour, until the English won, taking the town. The two commanders were among the very large number of casualties and both died of their wounds.

Efforts to recapture Quebec City failed and French rule in Canada ended with the Treaty of Paris of 1763. The only subsequent threat to English rule was the abortive American attempts to do by force what they had not been able to do by propaganda during the early days of the Revolution. A company under Benedict Arnold was sent to take Quebec City and assure its support of the American revolutionary effort. On the last day of 1775, American forces attacked the Lower Town—plaques now mark the site of the battle—but were defeated and captured or forced to retreat.

After this Quebec City lived in peace and prospered from its merchandise and its trade: furs, oils, lumber, shipbuilding, tanneries, furniture and textiles. Many of these articles have

**QUEBEC CITY –
MIDTOWN**

now declined or disappeared but have been replaced by the modern industries of tourism and government administration. In fact, the Quebec government employs about 10 per cent of the city's half-million people.

City Sights

The celebrated castle-hotel, the **Château-Frontenac,** built in 1892 and owned by Canadian Pacific, has become the city's landmark; its register contains many world-famous names. Begin a tour of Old Quebec with a stroll on **Dufferin Terrace** (1838) and the **Promenade des Gouverneurs** (1960), scenic terraces built on the edge of the cliff in front of the Frontenac. The view of the Lower Town and its Place Royale, of the St. Lawrence and the suburb of Lévis on the far shore is splendid summer and winter. At the north end of the terrace is an 1898 statue to Samuel de Champlain by sculptor Paul Chèvre. South from the monument the Terrace joins the Promenade, which extends all the way along the walls of the Citadel to Battlefields Park. Right next to the Château-Frontenac, the Jardin des Gouverneurs is a peaceful patch of greenery lined with old mansions, many of which have been converted to small hotels and *pensions.*

On the north side of the Château-Frontenac the **Place d'Armes** lies in the great shadow cast by the hotel. Here is the center of Old Quebec, once the garrison's training ground (hence the name) and its most important public square. You'll find a wax museum here, as well as the **Musée du Fort,** in which a scale model of Quebec City is used to bring to life the great battles of its past. The Monument to the Faith (*Monument de la Foi*) in the center of Place d'Armes pays tribute to the men who brought and spread the religion of France to the New World. On the Place d'Armes, you can hire a *calèche* (carriage) or, in winter, a sleigh, to take you on a 45-minute tour of the city's historical sights.

Descending to the north rim of the escarpment, you pass the **Quebec Seminary** buildings (1663), founded by the first bishop of Quebec, Mgr. François de Laval-Montmorency, and opened to students other than Jesuits in 1765. In the

Old Quebec snuggles at the foot of fairytale Château Frontenac.

summertime, open-air concerts are often held in the courtyard here, but if you're not lucky enough to be around for a concert, you can visit the seminary's chapel. Adjoining the seminary is **Notre-Dame Basilica,** first built in 1647 but ravaged several times by fire; the building you see is a 1922 restoration.

Other buildings in the old style on this side of town are the Crémazie House on the Rue de la Fabrique, home of the famous Canadian poet, the Carnet House, at the corner of Saint-Flavien and Couillard, named for the French Canadian historian who gave French Canadians a full sense of their identity by writing his *Histoire du Canada,* and the Touchet House at the intersection of Sainte-Famille and Hébert, nearly two centuries old and with a very French air about it.

Through the city walls and down the side of the escarp-

ment you'll reach Quebec's Lower Town and the Place Royale, almost directly beneath the Château-Frontenac. Here is the route that Benedict Arnold and his American forces followed to attack Lower Town. After the American defeat, captured American officers were trooped up the hill to the Quebec Seminary and held there as prisoners of war.

The **Place Royale** is the site of Champlain's very first settlement in Quebec and was the center of Quebec life from 1608 till 1759, when during the great siege of Quebec the English cannons damaged many of the old buildings and set others

Sunny Dufferin Terrace offers dominating views of town and river.

Whatever your style, you'll find inspiration in the charm of old Quebec.

afire. This holocaust in the defenseless Lower Town prompted many of the wealthy merchants who had made their fortunes on the river to move to Upper Town, where the new English rulers of Quebec were building strong defenses. During the later 19th and early 20th **68** centuries, the ancient buildings were often razed to make way for the warehouses, repair shops and other businesses which invaded the waterfront. But recently the area surrounding Place Royale has undergone extensive and painstaking restoration to bring back its 17th-century aspect, with very successful results.

Place Royale's name is due to the bust of Louis XIV in the center of the square. The present version (1931) is a replacement for the original erected in 1686, the 43rd year of Louis' 72-year reign.

Notre-Dame-des-Victoires is an attractive small stone church facing the square. Though built in 1688, it had to be restored after the 1759 bombardment. Ignoring the defeat, the Canadians gave it a name to recall two earlier French victories over the English, in 1690 and 1711.

Of the many excellently restored houses and shops in the Lower Town, don't miss the **Chevalier House,** an odd grouping of several distinct but adjoining houses with old Quebec furniture; see also the **Fornell House,** home of the Maison des Vins (see p. 98), which has opened its cellars to visitors and the house of Louis Joliet, the great Quebec-born explorer and fur trader who, along with Jacques Marquette, explored the Mississippi River all the way to its confluence with the Arkansas, several thousand miles from Quebec. (His name was given to a town in Illinois.) Joliet's house today is the lower terminus of the funicular which takes you up to Dufferin Terrace.

At the top of the terrace is the Place d'Armes. From this square, the Rue Saint-Louis heads southwest past some of Quebec's grandest modern buildings. The **Ursuline Convent,** a huge complex covering 7 acres, was founded in 1639, but has been rebuilt several times following decimation by fires. Several blocks farther along, the Parc de l'Esplanade offers a restful field of green shade along the city walls. You'll find the office of tourism for the Quebec Urban Community in the park.

The **Citadel** is an impressive monument approached up a hill and through a stone-lined tunnel. The original French fortifications here are topped by the British version (1820) which took 30 years to complete. The fortress was manned by British troops for a mere 20 years before the garrison was replaced by Canadian troops. The Changing of the Guard (10 a.m. daily, mid-June to Labor Day) and Beating the Retreat (7 p.m. on Tuesdays, Thursdays, Saturdays and Sundays) are colorful additions to Citadel life. The Military Museum, housing trophies of the Citadel's Royal 22nd Regiment, also has scenes and artifacts from early Quebec and a brilliant display of **69** military costumes. Except for the Changing of the Guard and Beating the Retreat ceremonies, visits to the Citadel are by guided tour only. March to October, tours are scheduled every day; February and November, only on weekdays; in December and January the Citadel is closed to visitors.

Can it be the "Cariboo" (see box, right) that fires ice sculptors' imagination for Quebec carnival?

Through the St. Louis Gate, the area to the right along the city walls is the center of carnival activity in February. Across Avenue Dufferin are the parliament buildings of the Quebec National Assembly erected in 1886 in the 17th-century French style. Nearby, the modern buildings housing other government offices attest to the progressive spirit of Quebec's citizens and planners.

Rue Saint-Louis turns into the Grande-Allée and con-

tinues past the parliament buildings to skirt **Battlefields Park** with the Plains of Abraham. The provincial **Museum** in the park is a treasurehouse of Quebec history with displays of coins, architectural models, historical documents and, of particular interest, a great collection of the carved wooden figures for which the province is famous. The museum is open Monday, Tuesday, Thursday and Friday from 9 a.m. to 5 p.m., Wednesday from 9 a.m. to 11 p.m., Sunday from 11 a.m. to 5 p.m.

On the way back to the center of Old Quebec from Avenue Turnbull, you'll see **Le Grand Théâtre,** the city's arts center and a symbol of the New Quebec, inaugurated in 1970.

Carnival in Quebec
In the pre-Lenten season, the people of Quebec throw off their normal decorum to indulge in a little mid-winter madness. The dates change with the church calendar, but sometime in February, the dreariest month of the long winter, the quiet park facing the National Assembly becomes the Place du Carnaval, featuring a huge Ice Palace. Fanciful, comic or dramatic ice sculptures of gigantic proportions are carved here, decorating the "palace square." Hardly simple snowmen, these are highly competent works of art. The only snowman is Bonhomme Carnaval, the jovial spirit of this February fun, always portrayed with a red *tuque* (cap) and a colorful Indian herringbone sash.

Two weekends and the week in between are hectic with activities: hockey tournaments, the coronation of the Carnival Queen, fireworks, a canoe race on the icy St. Lawrence, formal dances and general celebrations. The two parades attract crowds of merry revelers, who careen along behind the floats and bands. Fighting the frigid weather, trumpet-players carry and play their instruments in special muffs so the valves won't freeze. Onlookers keep warm by sipping a lethal liquid called "Cariboo" (sweet red wine and whiskey or grain spirits), sometimes sold in plastic Carnival "canes" and "trumpets". "The party" warms up as the canes get lighter.

The Night Parade on the Saturday before the end of Carnaval is the grand finale, and city hotels are booked to capacity as special trains bring hundreds of revelers from Montreal to share in the excitement. If you go, make advance hotel reservations.

What to Do

The Museums

The **Museum of Fine Arts** (*Musée des Beaux-Arts*) at 1379 Sherbrooke Street West (Metro: *Guy*), has a well-balanced collection of art from ancient times to the 20th century, arranged by period and geographical area. There's something for everyone, which makes the museum a very popular place. European painting is well represented, with the latest Rubens acquisition (1975) taking place of pride. There are ancient works from the Middle East, Greece, Rome and the Islamic countries and African masks and statues, but the museum's best showpieces are the pre-Columbian figures. Canadian paintings and furniture, and Innuit (Eskimo) figures and artifacts are also on display. You can buy a museum guidebook at the entrance or a less expensive brochure including a directory of the collections and a plan of the recently modernized and expanded museum building. The museum is open daily except Mondays from 11 a.m. to 5 p.m.

McGill University's **McCord Museum,** 690 Sherbrooke Street West (Metro: *McGill*), offers a colorful display of Canadian and Eskimo objects. The emphasis is on artifacts from the history of Canada, including a full-size totem pole and a collection of fascinating pictures of early Canadian life. The McCord is open from Wednesday through Sunday from 11 a.m. to 5 p.m.

The **Post Office House** (*La Maison de la poste*), 640 St. Catherine Street West. Exceptionally well organized, the museum offers a complete range of Canadian stamps and at the same time a good opportunity to get acquainted with the stamp production. You can see stamp blocks, corner blocks, first-day covers, complete panes, special albums, mounting sheets. Whenever it's a stamp issue day, activity is at its most hectic. An experienced staff is willing and able to help at all times on any philatelic problem.

The **Museum of Contemporary Art** (*Musée d'Art Contemporain*) down by the harbor, is reached by car, taxi or bus No. 12, which you take along University Street from Place Bonaventure to Cité du Havre. The museum is open every day but Monday. Besides a permanent collection of works by Quebec, and other Canadian artists (including an interesting collection of Canadian wood sculpture), the museum features temporary exhibits—from photography, painting, textiles or sculpture to any of the other varied traditional or off-beat media used today. One room in the museum is devoted to the paintings of Paul-Emile Borduas (1905–60), the boy from rural Quebec who became one of Canada's major abstract painters.

The **Canadian Historical Museum** (*Musée Historique Canadien*) is actually a wax museum. This privately run gallery shows 200 figures arranged in scenes portraying events in the Bible, and in Canadian and modern history.

Before the settlers: preserved in the McCord Museum, Indian artifacts, tomahawks, tunics record a way of war and peace from another century.

The sinuous darkened hallways lead through a model of the catacombs of Rome, explaining the life and trials of the early Christians, the founding of Montreal by Maisonneuve and a number of other portrayals of momentous events. The costumes are of as much interest as the wax figures and can be very rich and elaborate. Guided tours in French or English are available; the museum is open every day, and is located near the St. Joseph Oratory; take the Metro to Snowdon.

Some magnificent railway coaches (once owned privately by multi-millionaires) are shown at the **Canadian Railway Museum;** it also exhibits streetcars, quaint locomotives and other railway memorabilia. Located in the Montreal suburb of St. Constant, it displays over 100 cars and engines from all periods of railroad history and you can even ride in one—each week-

day a streetcar takes visitors on a short run; on Sundays they even stoke up one of the old trains for a short trip into nostalgia. The museum is open daily in summer only.

The **Dow Planetarium** (Metro: *Bonaventure*), several blocks southwest of Place Bonaventure, has interesting shows in English every afternoon and evening except Monday. The current show is usually advertised in the entertainment section of *The Gazette,* or phone 872-4530 for information.

A bookshop in the lobby sells publications on astronomy as well as scientific games.

For a change of pace, visit old Quebec by calèche. *Or try Montreal's Fine Arts Museum for its superb collection of pre-Columbian figures.*

Shopping

Montrealers love to shop, and no wonder. The choice of goods in the temptingly full shops is overwhelming and each new shopping area a cause of real excitement. Canada's close links with France, famed for its elegant women, and England, known for its well-dressed men, have led to a veritable cornucopia of stores ranging from branches of leading London shops to windows dressed with displays that rival Parisian boutiques.

The Old Guard in shopping are the large department stores on St. Catherine Street, many of which have been here for over a hundred years. Ogilvy's, 1307 St. Catherine West, was founded when the Scots were lords of Montreal's business world, and every day at 12, a bagpiper goes the rounds of the five floors, piping merrily.

Next of the Old Guard is Simpson's, which is not, like its London namesake, a large clothing store catering mainly to men, but rather a complete department store (between Mansfield and Metcalf on St. Catherine). It's a comfortable, faintly Anglo-Saxon store which sells just about everything including some things you don't need but may greatly

desire, such as Cuban cigars. The Dunhill Humidor, on the main floor near the Metcalf Street entrance, stocks its large climate-controlled cabinet with many varieties of Cuban, Jamaican and other fine cigars, cigarettes and pipe tobaccos from around the world.

Eaton's (St. Catherine at University), is somewhat like Simpson's: practical, and selling products which are good value for money. New Yorkers might think of it as "Montreal's Macy's" as it is the city's largest store.

Another store is run by the Hudson's Bay Company, the famed company founded to exploit Canada's fur wealth. Called the Bay (or *La Baie*), at St. Catherine between Union and Aylmer, it sells everything but is most famous for its furs and fur products, of course. Fur or leather coats are almost *de rigueur* in Montreal, both from the standpoint of fashion and that of practicality. Furs are not exactly cheap here except during the price-blasting sales. And a fur coat can be restyled and tailored to suit changing fashions. Used fur coats may

Undecided between rustic handicrafts and Paris haute couture? Try top-quality English fabrics.

sell for a few hundred dollars; new coats cost, of course, considerably more, depending on the type of fur and style.

Finally, Montreal's last word for high fashion—and high prices—is Holt Renfrew, the very posh store at 1300 Sherbrooke West, two blocks from St. Catherine. The latest Parisian fashions appear quickly in Holt's plushy displays, as do the customers to buy them.

All of these large department stores have branches throughout the city, sometimes large, sometimes small, often located in the subterranean shopping complexes.

For interesting boutiques, used goods, antiques, craft items and, in general, the kinky shops that come and go quickly, go to Crescent Street and its two neighbors, Mountain and Bishop Streets, between St. Catherine and Sherbrooke. Also, keep your eye out for shops selling such items during your stroll through Old Montreal, for St. Paul Street has its share of these shops, too. You will find a few similar shops on Saint-Denis (Metro: *Berri-de Montigny*), between Maisonneuve Boulevard and Marie-Anne Street, as well as on Prince Arthur Street and Duluth Avenue on the Mount Royal plateau.

Local Crafts

Products of Quebec craftsmen and artisans are sold in several large specialty stores. The largest selection of crafts may be found in stores called "Le Rouet". The biggest is on Ste-Catherine between University and McGill. The branch in Old Montreal is open late from Thursdays to Saturdays. For last-minute buys, try the duty-free section of Mirabel airport. Here are some shopping ideas:

Quebec carved wooden figures, an old traditional art; the wizened and bent old men always have a jovial, cheerful look as though they know the secret of a happy old age (is it being a woodcarver?). There's great variation from the very rough to the quite refined, that's reflected in the price.

Rag dolls, variations on the "Raggedy Ann" design.

Patchwork quilts make excellent gifts—if a bit pricey.

Indian moccasins, the real thing, practical and colorful.

Mukluks, the bulky fur-and-sealskin boots that keep an Eskimo fisherman's feet warm in the Arctic ice.

Eskimo soapstone (steatite) carved figures, vary colossally in artistry and in price.

Eskimo pipes, with wooden stems and soapstone bowls,

which look like Indian "peace pipes".

Traditional Quebec carved wooden figures waiting patiently together for a home of their own. Yours?

Snowshoes, authentic wood and gut, very durable.

Prints, on rice paper done by well-known Eskimo artists; each print is titled, signed and dated in English or French as well as in Eskimo runes. Most are collectors' items.

Baskets, birchbark and wicker or grass.

Traditional wooden furniture, rag carpets and hand-woven textiles are also on display.

Another place to buy craft items is the Canadian Guild of Crafts, 2025 Peel Street. Here, Eskimo carvings in steatite, calcite and serpentine with ivory accents are displayed in glass cases; the selection is limited and very fine. Modern textiles usually also have a prominent place in the Guild's window, as do a variety of other items including quaint little wooden molds in the shape of a maple leaf for making maple-sugar candy.

There's a nice little museum in an upstairs rear gallery featuring a selection of outstanding craft items. **79**

Outdoor Markets

In summertime Montreal's outdoor food markets are bustling, full of color and tempting smells. The city's largest is in the heavily Italian neighborhood near the Metro's Jean-Talon station. From the station walk southwest on Avenue Jean-Talon, and after two blocks go southeast to Mozart Street. Market specialties include most of the things you'd find in a similar market in Genoa or Pisa, but the produce is from the rich countryside of Quebec.

Another outdoor market, closer to downtown, is the one on Atwater Avenue, near the Metro stop of the same name. Both markets are open Monday to Saturday in summer (the indoor part of Atwater market is open all year round).

The early-birds who show up at seven in the morning get the first friendly smiles from the vendors, have the pick of the stalls' burdened shelves, but don't bargain much—with the day still ahead of them, vendors don't feel like cutting prices. Shoppers who arrive at 10:30 or 11 a.m. find the market area filled with people, great quantities of tomatoes, apples and chickens disappearing into shopping bags, and price competition among vendors getting heated. Late afternoon or Saturday evening shoppers who stay away until the market is near closing get the pick of the prices, but not of the goods.

A Boat Ride on the St. Lawrence

A great way to get out of town is a boat ride around the Port of Montreal, the islands and the St. Lawrence. Tour ships of Montreal Harbor Cruises Inc. *(Les Croisières du Port de Montréal)* depart for cruises in the port and the St. Lawrence several times a day between May and October from Victoria Quai, the northernmost wharf in Old Montreal, at the foot of Rue Berri. The classical cruise lasts $1\frac{1}{2}$ hours and will take you around the port and past Man and His World and the Olympic sites on Ile Sainte-Hélène, as well as near the first locks of the St. Lawrence Seaway. A bar for refreshments and snacks, plus a running commentary on the history and activities of the harbors and the sights of the city skyline and Old Montreal keep passengers entertained. You can also join the "Sunset Cruise", the "Love Boat Cruise" or the "Sunday Morning Champagne Brunch Cruise". For further details, call (514) 842-3871.

Sports

Montreal is sports-mad and dozens of different sports are played by amateur and professionals alike. Bowling on the green? Skeet shooting? Curling? All these and plenty of others keep Montrealers trim. Newspaper sports pages, both French and English, give information about the major sports. For the minor ones, telephone Sports Québec at 2521-3109. Here's a rundown on some of the popular sports you may want to look into:

Baseball: the Montreal Expos (National League) play about 80 home games a season in the Olympic Stadium. Tickets are sold through the computerized TRS (Ticket Reservation Service). Ask at your hotel for the location of the nearest TRS outlet.

Car Racing: the Canadian Grand Prix, a Formula One car race, is held yearly in June on Notre Dame Island at the entrance to the St. Lawrence Seaway.

Cycling: bicycle racing is a very French passion and very much alive in Montreal since the opening of the spectacular Olympic Vélodrome, right next to the Olympic Stadium (Metro: *Pie IX*). Constructed of Cameroon redwood, the track is almost a sixth of a mile long. As for amateur bicycling, downtown traffic is so dangerous and the city's hills are so tiring, that you'll see few bikes in town. But the province in general goes all out for two-wheeled exercise. Quebec claims to be second in the world in the statistics of bikes per capita.

Fishing: Quebec boasts of thousands upon thousands of lakes and streams and equivalent numbers of fish are caught in them annually. The variety of fish in Quebec is extensive: all sorts of trout, pike, walleye (the famous *doré* of Montreal restaurants), bass perch, muskellunge, and in some parts of the province, sturgeon and salmon.

Football: the Montreal Concordes now play to capacity crowds of up to 70,000 or more in the Olympic Stadium. August games are played in sweltering heat; the final game in November, often in a snowstorm.

Hockey: the Montreal Canadians *(Les Canadiens)* of the National Hockey League are the city's stars in the firmament of sports. From October to April the Forum (Metro: *Atwater*) is packed with cheering fans, and tickets are at a premium. Try to reserve places before you get to Montreal, for **81**

once you arrive it may be impossible to find them.

Horse Racing: harness racing (pacers and trotters) at the Blue Bonnets Raceway on Décarie Boulevard at Avenue Jean-Talon, all year round. The sport is well developed in Montreal and is worth going to watch.

Hunting: the big game in Quebec is moose, caribou, black bear and whitetail deer; fowl includes partridge, duck and Canadian goose. The province is divided into zones with different regulations governing each. Arrangements for a hunting trip are best made through one of the many outfitters who specialize in this service. Lists of outfitters, camping places, parks and reserves and regulations for game hunting, migratory bird hunting and fishing are all available from the Services des Renseignements Touristiques, Québec Tourism, 150 est, boulevard Saint-Cyrille, Québec, GIR 4Y3.

Sailing: the city has a dozen yacht clubs, and sails fill the St. Lawrence each summer day. For information, contact the Quebec Sailing Federation through the office of the leisure association of Quebec, at 252-3000.

Skating: rinks and ponds for ice-skating are all over the city in winter. Beaver Lake in Mount Royal Park is a favorite because of its woodland setting. For conditions at others, call the local leisure development office at 872-6211.

Skiing: conditions are billed as "the best in the East," the season is long and there are areas to suit all tastes. The two types of skiing, downhill *(ski alpin)* and cross-country *(ski de fond)* are often (but not always) found side-by-side. Even if you plan to visit only Montreal itself, bring your cross-country skis for a run through Mount Royal Park. Major ski regions are: the Laurentians, easily accessible by bus and expressway from Montreal, southern Quebec near the New York/ Vermont border, and the area around Quebec City. The Fédération Québécoise du Ski, 1415 est, Jarry, Montreal H2E 2Z7 (tel. (514) 374-2500) gives information on ski competitions and special events. For snow conditions, check the daily newspapers, radio and TV stations, or call any Quebec Tourism Office.

Snowshoeing: trails are usually laid out along with the cross-country skiing trails. The most exciting ones are in provincial parks.

Tennis: the City of Montreal operates numerous outdoor and indoor courts for residents and visitors alike. Contact the city's Sports and Leisure Service at 725-6451.

From the exhilarating pace of ice-hockey to a relaxing game of golf—Montrealers are all-rounders.

Nightlife

Montrealers are as keen about going out on the town as they are about shopping and the city is alive every night of the week, except perhaps Sunday. From the expensive discothèques and supper clubs of the downtown hotels to the erotic movie houses and topless bars of St. Catherine Street East, there's something for everyone.

There's also plenty of evening fun for the young, from movies in the underground city to discothèques at the top of skyscrapers. Every season there's a new "in" place (often the most recently opened), and long lines form at the door; some hopefuls never do see the inside. First-run movies are often mobbed, and crowds have to be organized with a loudspeaker. The secret is to go early.

Clubs and bars in the Crescent Street area often have ephemeral success, opening to hordes of the young and well-dressed, closing the next year as the crowd moves on. These small places often employ a "screener" who lets in only regulars or others who pass him a substantial tip ($5 or so), enough to let him know that more will be spent freely inside.

Though most of Montreal's theater activity is in French, the Centaur Theater in Old Montreal and the Saidye Bronfman Center have both traditional and experimental plays in English. Concert activity is centered on the Place des Arts for symphonic music and ballet, and the Forum for popular and rock. Newspapers and the city's

Warm up in the wintertime with **86** *authentic Quebec entertainment.*

Calendar of Events, issued free at hotels and tourist offices, have details of current entertainment.

The famous *boîtes à chansons* with their songs and ballads are now well on their way out and have been replaced largely by *cafés-théâtres,* cafés where theater performances are given. A real Quebec speciality, everyone can enjoy them—even if you can't make much of the thick Canadian dialect of French, *joual,* the nuances of which only a native will really appreciate.

For light entertainment on summer nights, there's a lot of impromptu music in the parks such as Lafontaine Park for all to enjoy, after which it's pleasant to go and have a drink at a terrace on Rue St-Denis or Prince Arthur.

Drinking Places

The *Québécois'* tavern is the last stronghold of the masculine world. Like a Mexican to his

cantina, the Quebecer goes to the tavern to unwind, not to be on his best behavior, and to further this aim women are excluded by law. These can be jolly or boisterous places if a hockey match is on the TV, but you may have to pick up a bit of the local French dialect before conversation comes easily.

A *brasserie* (literally, a brewery) is a more congenial place for out-of-town visitors to meet Montrealers or other travelers, and women are wel-comed with or without an escort. Though not really breweries, *brasseries* offer beer both in bottles and on tap *(bière en fût)* and also cider. *"Mets"* (meals) of the rough-and-ready variety are almost always offered, and the list may include an *assiette Québécoise* (Quebec plate) of pigs' knuckles, pork and beans, meatballs and

Unused to summer heat, music-lovers keep cool in the shade.

tourtière (meat-and-potato pie) with French fries (chips) at a reasonable price.

To see and be seen, you'll have to go to one of the pubs or bars on Crescent Street: shoulder your way in and then try to look as though you've been there forever. Though the Crescent Street pubs—some of which are authentically English—and the bars attract the young, affluent and beautiful, others in quieter districts are for the business set or the Irish dreaming of the "auld sod." The bars in the big hotels cater mostly to their guests and tend not to be very lively.

Festivals

Though local celebrations, fairs and festivals are held in various Quebec towns throughout the year (see also PUBLIC HOLIDAYS in the blueprint section of this book) the most famous and colorful are these:

Quebec Carnival (see p. 71), held for ten days beginning on the first weekend in February, is unparalleled for its mid-winter merriment. Every hotel room in town is booked in advance.

Carnaval-Souvenir de Chicoutimi is a celebration similar to the one in Quebec City and held for 10 days in February after the latter ends. Chicoutimi is about 150 miles north of Quebec City.

Eastern Townships Festival (*Festival des Cantons*), a rite of spring held for four days (Thursday to Sunday) at the end of May and beginning of June in the city of Sherbrooke (about 60 miles east of Montreal). The arts, music, crafts, games, feasts, and fireworks are all part of this celebration, which is symbolised by a weathercock. Festival participants light a candle each morning the festival is in progress and on Saturday night they're supposed to light it so that it burns at both ends, which gives you an idea of what the festival's all about.

St. John the Baptist Day (*Fête de Saint-Jean Baptiste*), June 24, is a day of carnival and merry-making in Montreal and other towns and cities of Quebec. Fireworks, dancing in the streets and special programs highlight the feast of the patron saint of French Canada. This is a uniquely *Québécois* celebration, not observed in other Canadian provinces.

The **Quebec Summer Festival** (*Festival d'été*) in July, with dancing, shows, parades and sports events, is gaining ever-greater popularity.

Wining and Dining

The French tradition of *haute cuisine* makes dining the day's most important activity. Combine this tradition with the Montrealers' love for a night on the town, and the result is a fairground of culinary delights. Restaurants range in price and quality from simple to sophisticated, and most Montrealers are willing to pay well to eat well. Note that a 10 per cent tax will be added to any meal check totalling over $ 3.50 and there is a tip in addition.

Breakfast: This hearty repast follows the American and British pattern: bacon and eggs (and the bacon is "back bacon," or "Canadian bacon" to outsiders), hot or cold cereals, or griddle cakes with *sirop d'érable* (maple syrup), toast and doughnuts *(beigne)* and coffee. Almost any coffee shop serving breakfast will have waitresses who understand your Franglais order for *deux œufs sunnyside-up*.

Refills on coffee are free in most places. Breakfast is served between about 7 and 11 a.m.

Lunch: The *déjeuner d'affaires*—businessman's lunch—is well established in Montreal restaurants. Though sometimes strictly *table d'hôte*, a fixed-price menu, there's often some

Outdoor cafés in cobbled streets; is this really in North America?

90

choice in the soup, main course and dessert courses. Besides the fixed menu, you can also have the à la carte luncheon with prices substantially lower than those for the same dishes on the dinner menu. Prime lunch hours are 12:30 to 2:30 p.m.

Dinner: Chefs save their prize recipes for the main per-formance, the evening meal. Service is generally polite and attentive, with little of the af-fectation sometimes associated with restaurants in the French tradition. Waiters are willing to help with meal and wine selection and, in fact, it is a good idea to ask what the chef may have as a specialty not on

the menu. Reservations are required and respected, punctuality is encouraged, and local etiquette demands that bookings be cancelled by phone if there's a change in plans. Restaurants open for dinner around 6:30 or 7 p.m., and often stay open till midnight or later. On Sundays these times are an hour or two earlier. There are, however, a good number of restaurants and cafés in Montreal where you can eat at any time of the day, and one or two operate round the clock. If a restaurant closes during the week, it is usually on Monday.

"Dinner and a show" is not the style in Montreal. The dinner *is* the show, the show an added extra—and one that shouldn't be rushed for.

Types of Restaurants

Deluxe: All the large downtown hotels have one or more restaurants, and most are patronized by Montrealers as well as visitors. Often there is a floorshow and/or dance band; the service is dignified, the wine cellar very good, and the menu tends to be the well-known rather than the *recherché:* frogs' legs in garlic butter *(cuisses de grenouille à l'ail),* tournedos of beef, and *coquilles Saint-Jacques* (scallops in cream sauce in a seashell, sprinkled with Parmesan cheese and baked). Every now and then moose or bear steak may be offered just to show this is Canada and not France. The word moose *(orignal* in French) may have a comical ring to it, but anyone who has tasted this sublimely tender and flavorful meat finds it hard to go back to beef. Prices in deluxe restaurants are high, the cost of wines very near exorbitant.

Small and cozy: Montreal has many small bistros where you'll find real culinary adventure. A few dishes from the classic French repertoire will always be available and Quebec produce will dictate the rest: fish from the lakes and rivers and meat dishes based mainly on pork. The Rue Saint-Denis area and the streets of Old Montreal abound with these gourmets' retreats.

Ethnic restaurants: The fourth dimension in Montreal dining, after French, *Québécois* and American, is the international one. Since the time when the first three types were established here, many new groups have immigrated to Montreal bringing their distinctive dishes, with excellent results: won ton soup, Portuguese octopus stew, moussaka and cannelloni are all readily

Casse-croûte

Casse-croûte ("break a crust") might be what was done for a snack years ago in France, but in Montreal today a *casse-croûte* is a snack bar or light lunch counter. Ham or grilled cheese sandwiches, plates of pork and beans, and *hot-dogs steamés* with *patates frites* (French fries, chips) are what satisfy the hunger here. *Casse-croûtes* can be anything from a curbside hot-dog vendor to small cafeterias, but they all have the means—both delicious and inexpensive—to cure a tourist's hunger pangs.

available, either in fine recipes that approach *haute cuisine*, or in robust, popular versions.

Sidewalk cafés. The coffee-house tradition has caught on in a big way in Montreal. In the past there were few streets with wide enough sidewalks for proper cafés; and also, Montrealers are so purposeful that they didn't go to a café simply to relax and do nothing. Now they've taken lessons from their cousins in Quebec City, who find it very easy to casually chat with friends over a coffee or beer. In summer, the best areas for sitting and dawdling are Rue Saint-Denis between Maisonneuve and Marie-Anne, and Place Jacques-Cartier in Old Montreal.

Montreal Cuisine

Here are the highlights of the city's varied menus:

Soups

The French classic onion soup is often served—and is often disappointing. Certain chefs assume it is simple to make, and end up with something that tastes more of salt or bouillon cubes than of onions. The *soupe aux pois*, made the Quebec way with yellow peas, is a much better bet. *Bouillabaisse* (fish chowder), different from its Mediterranean relative, is often outstanding.

Fish

Quebec is justly famed for its fish, both fresh- and salt-water. First among them is the *doré* (walleyed pike/perch), a fish of firm, white flesh and exquisite flavor. The best is the variety known as *doré noir;* somewhat less tasty, but still delicious, is the *doré jaune.* Prepared in many ways, it is usually served as a filet, perhaps *aux noisettes* (with hazelnuts).

The delicious selection of trout *(truite)* available in Montreal is second to none. Speckled, rainbow, brook trout and others may come poached or sautéed with almonds *(amandine)* in the classic manner of French cuisine.

Though *doré* and trout are the fish most seen on menus, many other fish, including seasonal sturgeon and salmon, are served in Montreal. Species of fish not native to Quebec waters are often shipped in bringing even more variety to the provincial bill of fare awaiting you in many restaurants.

Fowl

Chicken and turkey are common on Montreal menus, but the real stars are duck *(canard)* served with traditional orange sauce or maple syrup, a delectable variation, partridge, grouse and occasionally Canadian goose *(outarde)*.

Meat

Beef is always available, but pork is the basis of Québécois meat dishes, whether it be a piece of fatty bacon which flavors *fèves au lard* (pork and beans), or thick pork chops cooked in apple cider. Traditional favorites are pigs' feet, hocks or knuckles stewed or braised, hearty and full of flavor, or *andouillette aux fines herbes*, flavorful pork sausage sautéed with delicate spices. Less exotic are the *boulettes* (meatballs) stewed in a rich tomato sauce. The star of regional cuisine is *tourtière*, a meat pie which, to be authentic, must be made from venison, partridge, hare and finely chopped potatoes. More often these days it's made with pork, veal, chicken and minuscule bits of potato. It can range in quality from a hearty, full-flavored dish to a bland meat pie, often depending on what you pay for it. *Cipaille* is a similar pie, but layers of meat-and-potato filling alternate with six layers of pie crust. Finally, Quebec chefs (and housewives) make a kind of pâté called *cretons* from minced pork cooked with spices.

Montreal's big lunch dish is smoked meat sandwich *(sandwich de bœuf fumé)*. Large chunks of beef are spiced and smoked, then sliced, put between dark or light rye bread and garnished with dill pickle. The home stretch for this Canadian corned beef special is Boulevard Saint-Laurent near Square Saint-Louis. Each delicatessen here has its own variations of the sandwich, including one with an extraordinary outer coating of coriander seeds on the beef. Try it once, and you'll likely come back for more!

Salads

In true French tradition, salad is usually served as a separate course after the main course, but before the cheese, to clear the palate and aid digestion. Sometimes it is served American-style as a first course.

What Kentucky fried chicken is to an American, smoked meat and French fries is to a Montrealer.

Vinaigrette (oil, vinegar, garlic, salt and pepper) is a popular salad dressing, but the vinegar may well be from cider rather than wine as it is in France. Vinegar is also often used as a garnish for French fries (chips), instead of ketchup.

Cheese

A big selection of imported cheeses are offered in Montreal's restaurants and markets, but the great local cheese is made by Trappist monks in Oka, from which the cheese takes its name. With a fine white mold like Camembert or Brie, a well-aged Oka's texture slightly resembles fresh Munster; the flavor is somewhat stronger than Brie. It's delicious! And Quebec produces 50 more cheeses worth trying.

Desserts

French pastry is a favorite all over the city, but the regional specialty is maple sugar pie *(tarte au sucre),* a sweet, heavenly concoction of eggs, brown sugar, maple syrup, butter, chopped nuts, with a few drops of vinegar and a pinch of salt. It often comes with whipped cream, absolutely delicious and wicked for a diet. In season, tasty *tartes* are also made from *bleuets* (blueberries) and *pommes* (apples).

Cider, Wine, Beer—or Spirits?

"Cider" means many different things in Montreal. *Cidre* is not found in restaurants, but in *brasseries,* taverns and some cafés. Triple Six, a popular brand, is typical of *cidre léger* (light cider)—it comes in a soft-drink bottle and looks like effervescent mineral water. It's deliciously dry and tart, and has about the same alcoholic content as beer. Some other brands of effervescent cider come in brown bottles and are the golden color of apple juice.

Beer is drunk everywhere in Canada, and the large brewing companies (Molson, Labatt, O'Keefe and others) make beers similar but rather stronger than the American ones.

Wine is the most common drink with dinner, and though most of the wine consumed in Canada is imported from Europe, some locally made table wines are also on sale.

In restaurants, clubs and bars drinks are fairly expensive. If having wine, best specify a carafe rather than a bottle—this will bring its price

At day's end, Montrealers of both language communities enjoy relaxing French style—with good food.

down considerably, and the quality of open wines is usually quite presentable.

Beer and cider are sold in grocery stores which have licenses to sell them; supermarkets do not have such licenses.

Wines and liquors are also sold in grocery stores and by the Quebec Liquor Corporation *(Société des Alcools du Québec)*, a government-run distributor with stores dotted around the city, and in grocery stores. You can also get excellent wines at the Maison des Vins, located on Montreal's Avenue President Kennedy and on Quebec City's Place Royale.

Finally, at the end of the day, if the choice of one of the above drinks is too difficult to make, you can't go far wrong with a jigger of one of the finest whiskeys in the world—Canadian rye.

To Help You Order...

Could we have a table for..., please?
Do you have a set menu?

Nous voulons une table pour... personnes, s'il vous plaît.
Offrez-vous un menu table d'hôte?

I'd like a/an/some...

Je veux un/une/de...

beer	**bière**	mineral water	**eau minérale**
bread	**pain**	(effervescent)	**(gaseuse)**
butter	**beurre**	napkin	**serviette**
cider	**cidre**	pepper	**poivre**
coffee	**café**	potatoes	**patates, pommes**
dessert	**dessert**		**de terre**
fish	**poisson**	rice	**riz**
fork	**fourchette**	salad	**salade**
fruit	**fruit**	salt	**sel**
glass	**verre**	soup	**soupe, potage**
ice-cream	**crème glacée,**	spoon	**cuillère**
	glace	sugar	**sucre**
knife	**couteau**	syrup (maple)	**sirop (d'érable)**
meat	**viande**	tea	**thé**
menu	**menu, carte**	water (iced)	**eau (glacée)**
milk	**lait**	wine	**vin**

98

...and Read the Menu

agneau	lamb	**gâteau**	cake
aiglefin	haddock	**homard**	lobster
ail	garlic	**huîtres**	oysters
ananas	pineapple	**huile**	oil
artichaut	artichoke	**jambon**	ham
asperges	asparagus	**laitue**	lettuce
aubergine	eggplant	**langue**	tongue
beurre	butter	**lapin**	rabbit
biftek	beefsteak	**légumes**	vegetables
bleuets	blueberries	**lièvre**	hare
bœuf	beef	**morue**	cod
boulettes	meatballs	**moules**	mussels
brochet	pike	**moutarde**	mustard
canard	duck	**noix**	nuts
caneton	duckling	**nouilles**	noodles
champignons	mushrooms	**œufs**	eggs
chou	cabbage	**oie**	goose
choufleur	cauliflower	**oignons**	onions
citron	lemon	**orignal**	moose
concombre	cucumber	**ouananiche**	landlocked salmon
confiture	jam		
courge, courgette	zucchini squash, vegetable marrow	**ours**	bear
		pamplemousse	grapefruit
crevettes	shrimp	**pêches**	peaches
dinde	turkey	**poires**	pears
doré	pike/perch	**pommes**	apples
épinards	spinach	**poulet**	chicken
érable	maple (sugar or syrup)	**rognons**	kidneys
		saucisse	sausage
escargots	snails	**saumon**	salmon
faisan	pheasant	**tarte**	pie
fèves	baked beans	**tomate**	tomato
flétan	halibut	**tourtière**	meat-and-potato pie
foie	liver		
fraises	strawberries	**truite**	trout
framboises	raspberries	**veau**	veal
fromage	cheese	**venaison**	venison (deer steaks)

BLUEPRINT for a Perfect Trip

How to Get There

Because of the complexity and variability of the many fares, you should ask the advice of an informed travel agent well before your departure.

From the United States and Canada

BY AIR: There are non-stop flights from major Canadian and U.S. cities such as Winnipeg, Ottawa, Boston, Chicago, Miami and New York as well as daily direct flights with one or two stops from certain other major cities.

Excursion fares with savings up to 20 per cent are available from most U.S. cities.

BY RAIL: Coach rail fare is cheaper than air fare, especially if you buy a ticket for off-peak dates when rates are reduced. You can reserve sleeping accommodation on any of the three best trains to Montreal. The *Montrealer,* from Washington, D.C., offers an overnight trip both ways. The bar car is lively on weekends, and meals feature standard fare as well as French-Canadian specialties. Other Amtrak trains connect with VIA Rail Canada at Port Huron and Detroit or Fort Erie. From the Northwest the best train connections are made by going north and taking the transcontinental *Canadian* from Vancouver.

BY BUS: Even less expensive than the train, bus service is available from all parts of the United States to Montreal. The main company, Greyhound/Trailways, Inc., has frequent service to New York City with direct daily connections to Montreal, an eight-hour trip. From Boston, Vermont Transit has daily buses to Montreal.

BY CAR: Highways to Montreal are good from anywhere in the U.S. and Canada. From the northern or western U.S., the Trans-Canada Highway (Autoroute 17) provides an introduction to Canadian scenery if you have some extra time. Otherwise interstate highways through Chicago and Detroit link up with Canada's routes 401 and 20, which skirt Lakes Erie and Ontario and lead directly to Montreal. The major route from New York State and the Atlantic region is Interstate 87 which becomes Autoroute 15 at the Quebec border. New Englanders can use Interstates 89 or 91 to connect with the Canadian highways leading to Montreal.

From the United Kingdom

BY AIR: Scheduled flights leave London daily and Glasgow several times a week. There is a wide range of fares applying to Montreal flights, dependent upon the traveler's plans (length of stay), how long in advance you can book your ticket, as well as the normal seasonal variations in prices. July to September is the high season.

Most package tours take in Montreal along with other tourist areas. Tour operators use Advance Booking Charter (ABC) fares and add an organized package holiday. Charter flights from London also use ABC fares; book at least 21 days prior to departure, round-trip only (travel to one Canadian city and return from another is permissible). There is a vast range of fly-drive packages and other package tours.

From Australia, New Zealand and South Africa

Australia: Regular flights leave from Sydney with connections in Vancouver or Los Angeles. Package deals run by airlines are sometimes available, and excursion fares or APEX are advantageous.

New Zealand: Daily air services leave for Montreal from Auckland with connections in Los Angeles. There are APEX and Point-to-Point fares available.

South Africa: All scheduled flights leave from Johannesburg with connections in Europe. Many types of package deals are offered by different airlines, and APEX and Excursion fares are also obtainable.

When to Go

Summers in Montreal are similar to those in New England cities, and most visitors arrive during that period. Other seasons have their attractions, however: autumn with its brilliant foliage and apple-picking at the end of September, winter skiing from November to April, and maple sugar time in March and April.

The following chart gives average monthly temperatures in Montreal:

	J	F	M	A	M	J	J	A	S	O	N	D
°C	-9	-8	-2	5	13	19	22	20	15	10	3	-5
°F	16	18	29	41	55	67	72	68	59	50	37	23

Planning Your Budget

To give you an idea of what to expect, here is a list of average prices in Canadian dollars. They can only be approximate, however, as inflation creeps relentlessly up.

Airports. Mirabel-Dorval (non-stop inter-airport bus service) $9, public bus Mirabel-downtown $9, taxi $45–50, public bus Dorval-downtown $7, taxi $18–19.

Car rental. *Subcompact* $35–50 per day (with 150 free kilometres), 15¢ per extra km., $160–190 per week (with up to 1,400 free km.). *Station Wagons* $45–55 per day (with 100 km. free), 21¢ per extra km., $266–270 per week (with up to 1,400 free km.). Add 9% tax. Cut-rate rental: $12–19 per day, $85–142 per week.

Cigarettes. Canadian brands $3.50 for 25, U.S. $3.20 for 20, French $3.10 for 20.

Entertainment. Nightclub/discotheque $2–5 and up, cinema $5–6.50.

Hairdressers. *Man's* haircut $8–13. *Woman's* cut from $15, shampoo and blow-dry $15 and up, permanent wave $50–80.

Hotels and motels (double room per night). Luxury (6 fleurs-de-lys) $150 and up, comfortable (3 fleurs-de-lys) $50–95, motels $45–150 depending on category.

Intercity buses. Montreal–Quebec City (round-trip day excursion) $30.95, 7-day ticket $32.15. Montreal–Mont-Tremblant (round-trip) $31.20. Montreal–Ottawa return $42 (valid one month), one-day excursion fare $19.90. Montreal–Toronto one way $35,70, return $55.45, one-day excursion fare $44.

Meals and drinks. Breakfast from $3, lunch/dinner from $8, coffee/soft drinks $1, bottle of wine from $10, beer $2.50, cocktails from $4.50.

Public transportation (City of Montreal). Bus/metro ticket $1, book of 6 tickets $5.50 (children $2.50), monthly card for unlimited number of rides $29.75.

Taxis. Drop rate $2.00, plus 70¢ per km., waiting charge $15 per hour.

Trains. Montreal–Quebec, one way, $28, Montreal–Ottawa $16, Montreal–Toronto $51.

An A–Z Summary of Practical Information and Facts

> Listed after most main entries is an appropriate French translation, usually in the singular. You'll find this vocabulary useful when asking for information or assistance.
> For prices, refer to list on p. 103.

A

ACCOMMODATIONS—see **HOTELS**

AIRPORTS *(aéroport)*. Montreal is served by two international airports. Mirabel, 35 miles northwest of the city, opened in 1975, is one of the world's largest airports; most intercontinental flights depart and arrive here, while most North American flights use Dorval Airport, 13 miles southwest of the city. Both have full facilities including currency-exchange offices, car rental agencies and special direct hotel reservation telephone lines. There is a non-stop bus service between the two airports.

Bus transportation to Mirabel is operated by MIRACAR from a special downtown terminal next to the Hotel Queen Elizabeth. For information, phone 397-9999. For fares, see p. 103.

The Murray Hill company operates bus services between Dorval and some downtown hotels. For information, phone 937-5311.

Quebec City's airport, Sainte-Foy, has a limousine and a bus service with the Château-Frontenac as the downtown terminal.

On flights to the U.S.A., passengers go through U.S Customs as they check in for their flight (and not after they have landed in the U.S.A.).

Porter!	**Porteur!**
Taxi!	**Taxi!**
Where's the bus for...?	**Où est l'autobus pour...?**

B

BABYSITTERS *(garde d'enfants)*. Most of the big downtown hotels and many motels offer baby-sitting services (give the front desk at least two hours' notice). The city also has several baby-sitting agencies (see the Yellow Pages of the telephone directory).

Can you get me a babysitter for tonight?	**Pouvez-vous me trouver une garde d'enfants pour ce soir?**

BANKS and CURRENCY-EXCHANGE OFFICES *(banque; bureau de change)*. Standard banking hours are from 10 a.m. to 3 p.m., Monday through Friday, but several banks have branches or sidewalk teller-windows which stay open until 5 or 6 p.m., and also do business on Saturday mornings. Currency-exchange offices at the airports are open every day from 6:30 a.m. to 10:30 p.m.

European and other currencies are not willingly exchanged outside major centres; best have as much as possible of your money (cash, traveler's checks, etc.) in Canadian (or U.S.) dollars. See also CREDIT CARDS AND TRAVELER'S CHECKS.

When changing money or traveler's checks, ask for 1- to 20-dollar bills, which are accepted everywhere, as some establishments will refuse to accept larger banknotes.

I want to change some U.S. dollars/pounds.	**Je veux changer des dollars américains/livres sterling.**

BICYCLE RENTAL. Even if downtown Montreal is not the best of places to get round by cycle, you'll certainly enjoy miles of relatively empty cyclable roads in the area round Montreal.

You can rent a bike from any of the bicycle stores listed under "Bicycles-Renting" or "Bicyclettes-Location" in the Yellow Pages of the telephone directory.

The Canadian Hostelling Association (see YOUTH HOSTELS) organizes cycling tours through the most interesting areas and towns of the Eastern coast down into north Vermont.

BUSES—see PUBLIC TRANSPORTATION and INTERCITY BUSES

CALECHES—see GUIDES

CAMPING *(camping)*. The Parks Branch of the Quebec Government operates 60 campgrounds in the province, but there are also numerous private camping areas. Rates depend on the services and facilities

C offered. Advance reservations are not usually necessary at park campgrounds. Offices are open from 7 a.m. to 10 p.m. For all further information and prices, write to the Quebec Department of Tourism, Fish and Game, 150 Saint-Cyrille Boulevard East, Quebec, Que. G1R 4Y1.

May we camp here, please?	**Pouvons-nous camper ici, s'il vous plaît?**
We have a tent/a trailer (caravan).	**Nous avons une tente/une caravane.**

CAR RENTAL (*location de voitures*). Car rental agencies have desks at both Dorval and Mirabel airports. Competition among companies is spirited, and plenty of special offers or package arrangements are available (for rates, see p. 103).

Most credit cards are accepted; without a credit card, the customer is required to put down a deposit equivalent to the anticipated total rental cost plus 20 per cent. Some firms set a minimum age at 21, others 25. See also DRIVING.

CHEMISTS'—see **MEDICAL CARE**

CIGARETTES, CIGARS, TOBACCO (*cigarettes; cigares; tabac*). In Montreal, shops which sell tobacco products are called *tabagies*. Major tobacconists' carry a wide selection of brands in cigarettes, cigars and pipe tobacco, and it should be possible to find almost anything you want. Tobacco products tend to be slightly more expensive in Canada than in the U.S., and slightly less expensive than in Great Britain (see p. 103).

A pack of.../A box of matches, please.	**Un paquet de.../Une boîte d'allumettes, s'il vous plaît.**
filter tipped/without filter	**avec/sans filtre**
light/dark tobacco	**du tabac blond/noir**

CLOTHING. Though summer days are apt to be hot, you should have a sweater or jacket for the evening, even in mid-July. In late spring and early autumn, be prepared for cool days and chilly nights. Winter weather doesn't bother most Montrealers because they dress for it: waterproofed leather boots or galoshes are standard footwear for everyone all winter. Fur, leather or heavy wool overcoats are everyday winter-wear, and only someone who enjoys head colds will forget hat and scarf.

Montrealers tend to be stylish and careful in dress rather than informal. Many clubs, restaurants and nightspots require men to wear a coat and tie.

C

COMPLAINTS. The manager of any respectable hotel is always available to put right any customers' complaints. Otherwise, the municipal, provincial and national tourist offices may be helpful. Quebec's provincial tourist office (see TOURIST INFORMATION OFFICES) acts rapidly on complaints about any establishment which may have overcharged or given bad service. Taxi companies will also take up any complaints about one of their drivers, but you'll have to know the driver's name and identification number (it will be on display in the cab).

Montreal has an official office, CIDEM, to handle complaints about commercial establishments, at

155 Notre-Dame Street East (tel.: 872-6010).

CONSULATES *(consulat)*

In Montreal:

American Consulate-General: Place Desjardins, Montreal; tel.: (514) 281-1886. Hours: 8:30 to 11:30 a.m. and 2 to 3:30 p.m., Monday through Friday.

British—Trade Commission and Information service*: 635 Dorchester Boulevard West, Montreal; tel.: (514) 866-5863. Hours: 9 a.m. to 5 p.m., Monday through Friday.

In Quebec City:

American Consulate-General: 1 Sainte-Geneviève, Quebec; tel.: (418) 692-2095. Hours: 8:30 a.m. to 12:15 p.m. and 1:45 to 4 p.m., Monday through Friday.

British—Information Office*: 500 Grande-Allée East, Suite 707, Quebec; tel.: (418) 525-5187. Hours: 9 a.m. to 5 p.m., Monday through Friday.

Apart from the consulates and information offices listed above, the principal embassies of the U.S., Britain, Ireland, Australia, New Zealand and South Africa are to be found in Ottawa.

CONVERTER CHARTS. Quebec uses the metric system for most computations, English and American measurements for others. The

---

* Perform the functions of a consulate.

107

C

aim is to convert completely to the metric system. In any case, nowa-
days weather reports, distances by main road, fuel, groceries, clothes,
etc., are given in metric measurements (or, in the latter two cases, in
both metric and old measurements).

Temperature

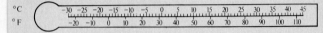

Length

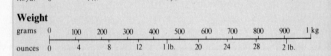

Weight

grams	0	100	200	300	400	500	600	700	800	900	1 kg
ounces	0	4	8	12	1 lb.	20	24	28	2 lb.		

For fluid measures, see p. 111.

CREDIT CARDS and TRAVELER'S CHECKS *(carte de crédit;
chèque de voyage).* The major credit cards and traveler's checks issued
in Canadian or U.S. dollars are accepted throughout Canada at
banks, hotels, restaurants, most shops and gas stations. Users of
various credit cards can also get cash, in Canadian dollars, round the
clock, from widely available dispensers. For transactions with credit
cards or traveler's checks, it's useful to have some form of identification. See also BANKS.

Do you accept traveler's checks?	**Acceptez-vous les chèques de voyage?**
Can I pay with this credit card?	**Est-ce que je peux payer avec cette carte de crédit?**

CRIME and THEFTS. As in all big cities precautions should be taken
in public places: pickpockets operate in crowded markets, on buses and
in the Metro; never leave objects in view in the car; always lock your
hotel room; deposit valuables in the hotel safe.

All in all, Montreal is a relatively safe place to walk around in; naturally, however, single people would do well to avoid run-down areas at night. See also POLICE.

CURRENCY. The Canadian dollar (abbreviated CAD outside Canada, to distinguish it from other dollars) is printed in both English and French; all bills are the same size, but the several denominations are of different colors.

Coins: 1, 5, 10, 25 and 50 cents and 1 dollar.

Bills: 1, 2, 5, 10, 20, 50, 100, 500 and 1,000 dollars.

In English, the Canadian names of the coins are the same as the American: cent, nickel, dime, quarter, half-dollar. In French, the words are:

cent	= *sou*	quarter	= *vingt-cinq sous*
nickel	= *cinq sous*	half-dollar	= *cinquante sous*
dime	= *dix sous*		

CURRENCY EXCHANGE—see **BANKS**

CUSTOMS CONTROLS *(douane)*. See also ENTRY FORMALITIES and AIRPORTS. The following chart shows what main duty-free items you may take into Canada and, when returning home, into your own country:

Into:	Cigarettes		Cigars		Tobacco	Spirits		Wine
Canada	200	and	50	and	900 g.	1.1 l.	or	1.1 l.
Australia	200	or	250 g.	or	250 g.	1 l.	or	1 l.
Eire	200	or	50	or	250 g.	1 l.	and	2 l.
N. Zealand	200	or	50	or	½ lb.	1 qt.	and	1 qt.
S. Africa	400	and	50	and	250 g.	1 l.	and	1 l.
U.K.	200	or	50	or	250 g.	1 l.	and	2 l.
U.S.A.	200	and	100	and	*	1 l.	or	1 l.

* a reasonable quantity

There's no limit to the amount of currency that can be imported or exported without declaration.

I've nothing to declare.	**Je n'ai rien à déclarer.**
It's for personal use.	**C'est pour mon usage personnel.**

DRIVING IN CANADA

U.S. visitors taking their cars into Canada will need:

● a valid U.S. driver's license
● car registration papers
● a Canadian Non-Resident Interprovince Motor Vehicle Liability Insurance Card or evidence of sufficient insurance coverage to conform with local laws (available from your insurance agent)

Cars registered in the United States can be brought into Canada by the owner or his authorized driver for up to a year by filling out a form at the border. U.S. auto insurance is usually valid in Canada; if in doubt, consult your agent. Note that if you rent a car in the U.S. to drive to Canada, at the border you'll have to show the rental contract, which must state that the car is intended for use in both Canada and the U.S.A.

European visitors taking their car to Canada will need:

● a valid driving license
● car registration papers
● third-party insurance

For temporary importation of your car (up to six months), no special customs documents are necessary. But after that, you'll have to pass the Canadian driving test.

Driving conditions: Regulations are similar to those in the U.S.: drive on the right, pass on the left, yield right of way to vehicles coming from your right at unmarked intersections. Roads in the province of Quebec are generally very good, with enough highway markers and directional signs to make finding your way easy. Montreal is well served by *autoroutes* (superhighways, motorways) from the New York border, from the Eastern Townships, from Quebec City and from the Laurentians, as well as several others. Maximum speed on expressways is 100 kilometres per hour (60 m.p.h.), on normal country roads 90 k.p.h. (56 m.p.h.), inside towns 50 k.p.h. (30 m.p.h.), and in school districts 30 k.p.h. (20 m.p.h.). The use of seat belts is obligatory in the province of Quebec.

Driving in Montreal: There are two million cars in Quebec. Montreal gets off to a sluggish start in the morning, but around noon all those cars seem to seek parking space in the same street.

The general rule for driving in Montreal is: take care. Look out for other cars; they won't look out for you. Beware of strange turning habits, swerving from lane to lane and drag-strip starts when the traffic light changes to green. In Montreal, driving is fast, spirited—and dangerous.

Parking: Street parking is regulated by dual-language signs (if you see only French, look on the reverse of the sign for the English). Private parking lots *(terrains de stationnement)* are expensive, municipal parking lots more reasonably priced, but crowded. Tow-away zones are called *zones de remorquage/touage.* Never park in front of a fire hydrant.

Drinking and driving: The police have the legal right to put you through a breath-analysis test. If the alcohol content is above 0.08 per cent, you're in trouble. If you couldn't resist one more glass of the local brew, you can always ask *a policeman* to drive you home! In Montreal, he is sure to oblige, or so the tourist offices tell you.

If you are carrying open bottles of wine or beer, it's wise to leave them in the trunk (boot).

Breakdowns: You'll hardly ever have any problem in locating a garage and spare parts to fix your car, whatever the make. In the city, the tourist office in Place Ville-Marie (see TOURIST INFORMATION OFFICES) will help you to find a garage. The *autoroutes* are patrolled by cars as well as by small planes—look out for the plane and make a signal if you've had a breakdown.

Fuel and oil: There are plenty of filling stations *(postes d'essence)* throughout Quebec. Gasoline *(essence)* comes in three types: regular *(régulier)*, unleaded *(sans plomb)* and premium *(extra/super)*. Fuel is sold by the liter.

Note that Quebec has many self-service gas stations *(libre service)*, and if you want to have an attendant fill the tank, check the oil and clean the windshield, look rather for a station with the sign *essence avec service* (gasoline with service).

Fluid measures

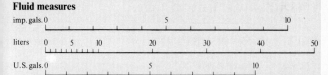

Road signs: Most road signs are both in French and English, or are self-explanatory symbols. If you do, however, find yourself in an exclusively French-speaking area, here are the most common written ones:

Arrêt	Stop
Attention	Caution
Cédez	Yield, give way

D

Défense de stationner	No parking
Ecole/Ecoliers	School/Students
Lentement	Slow
Piétons	Pedestrians
Réparations	Road work
Sortie de camions	Truck/lorry exit
Stationnement	Parking

(international) driving license	**permis de conduire (international)**
car registration papers	**les enregistrements du véhicule**
insurance card	**certificat d'assurance**
Are we on the road to...?	**Sommes-nous sur la route de...?**
Fill the tank, please.	**Faites le plein, s'il vous plaît.**
regular/premium	**régulier/super**
Check the oil/tires/battery.	**Vérifiez l'huile/les pneus/l'accu.**
I've had a breakdown.	**J'ai eu une panne.**
There's been an accident.	**Il y a eu un accident.**

DRUGS. Montrealers don't have much time for narcotics; most students seem more interested in sports and politics than in hash and dope. Police and narcotics agents do not prowl the streets and hotel corridors seeking out offenders, but customs men have their eyes, ears and noses (and sometimes their dogs' noses) set to gather evidence. If they catch a holiday-maker with illegal drugs, chances are he'll spend more than just his vacation with them.

DRUGSTORES—see **MEDICAL CARE**

DRY CLEANING—see **LAUNDRY**

E

ELECTRIC CURRENT. The current is the same as in the U.S.A.—110–120-volt, 60-cycle AC. Plugs are the standard two-flat-prong American type, so Europeans should buy a plug adapter before they leave for Canada.

an adapter (transformer)	**un adaptateur (transformateur)**
a battery	**une batterie**

112 EMBASSIES—see **CONSULATES**

EMERGENCIES. One central number handles all emergency calls, to police, fire and ambulance services: Dial 911.

Additional numbers for assistance:

Social Services:	931-2292
Distress Centre:	935-1101
Poison Control Centre:	1-800-463-5060

ENTRY FORMALITIES. See also CUSTOMS CONTROLS. U.S. citizens must have some type of identification and proof of address (voter registration card, birth certificate or passport) to show both the Canadian officials when entering and the U.S. officials when returning. A driver's license is not accepted as identification. British subjects and citizens of most Commonwealth and European countries as well as of Australia and New Zealand need only a valid passport—no visa—to enter Canada. But you could be asked at customs to show a return ticket and to prove that you have $20–30 for each day of your stay.

FASHION—see CLOTHING

GUIDES *(guide)*. A pleasant way to take the tour is in a *calèche* (horse-drawn carriage). Some *calèche* drivers and taxi drivers are licensed city guides and will show you Montreal. Ask for a driver in Dominion Square in Old Montreal, or on Mount Royal near Beaver Lake. Private guide service, paid by the hour, is also available at a similar fee. Contact the tourist office in Place Ville-Marie (see TOURIST INFORMATION OFFICES) for help in locating a guide.

HAIRDRESSERS' *(coiffeur)*. The large hotels all have good barbers *(barbier)* and hairdressers, often offering their service at prices comparable to those charged elsewhere in the city. For their rates, see p. 103. Tip from 12 to 15 per cent, but never less than $2.

haircut	**coupe**
shave	**rasage**
shampoo and blow-dry	**shampooing et brushing**
color rinse/tint	**shampooing colorant/teinture**

113

color chart	**carte de couleurs**
permanent wave	**permanente**
Not too much off (here).	**Ne coupez pas trop (ici).**
A little more off (here).	**Coupez un peu plus (ici).**

HITCH-HIKING *(auto-stop)*. Between cities it's possible to thumb a ride *(faire du pouce)*, though rides tend to be somewhat infrequent. However, with a backpack, heading for the Laurentians, your chances of being picked up are better than average.

HOTELS and ACCOMMODATIONS *(hôtel; logement)*. The Quebec Department of Tourism, Fish and Game (see TOURIST INFORMATION OFFICES) rates most establishments in the province and publishes these ratings. To do so, it uses a *fleur-de-lys* symbol, instead of stars, to indicate quality (5–6 *fleurs-de-lys* for a luxury hotel, 3–4 for a mid-range one, and 1–2 for a budget establishment). This directory, entitled *Accommodations Québec*, is available free at all tourist offices. Though hotels listed in the directory are required to have prices posted on an official rate card in each room, the government does not control prices (for average price of all accommodations, see p. 103). For information on bed and breakfast establishments, write to Montreal Bed & Breakfast, 4912 Victoria, Montreal H3W 2N1.

Luxury hotels: In the large luxury hotels, the price structure is complex. If demand is heavy, full prices are charged; but when business is slack, you may be able to get accommodation at specially advantageous rates. Package tour arrangements booked in advance are often granted very attractive reductions, sometimes up to 30 per cent. Weekend discounts and family tariffs are usually also available if you make advance reservations.

Mid-range: Smaller hotels and tourist homes *(maison de logement)* do not normally grant discounts except for groups or longer stays (a week or more), but the rooms, always clean and neat, may be more interesting, and service will be more personal in this type of hotel.

Budget: Inexpensive, simple hotels and rooming houses are scattered throughout the city. Rooms may be small, with only a washbasin and bath down the hall, and service may be minimal, but prices are truly advantageous—about half those of the mid-range hotels.

Motels are rated by the same criteria as hotels, and prices are in the same range. See also YOUTH HOSTELS.

INTERCITY BUSES. For rates, see p. 103. Montreal's intercity bus terminal is called Terminus Voyageur, the name of the principal company which uses it (corner Maisonneuve/Berri). From this terminal, Voyageur buses depart for Quebec City and the Laurentians as well as for Vermont and New York. Buses to Quebec City run every hour on the hour. Several a day leave the terminal for Mont-Tremblant in the Laurentians. For full schedule information, telephone the terminal at 842-2281.

Southern provincial traffic is handled from the Terminus Rive Sud (Metro: Longueuil) on the south shore of the St. Lawrence.

In Quebec City, the central bus terminal is at the Gare Centrale (Central Station) on Charest Boulevard.

See also PUBLIC TRANSPORTATION and TRAINS.

LANGUAGE. Though Montreal once had as many English-speakers as French, today it's estimated that two-thirds of the city's inhabitants speak French as their mother tongue. Of course, many French-speakers know English, or are even fully bilingual. Because French and English live so closely together in Montreal, a good many words pass from one language to the other and vice-versa: *autoroute* has come into the English vocabulary for superhighway/motorway, while "hot-dog" has replaced the French word *saucisse*.

Quebec French as spoken on radio and TV is, of course, fully comprehensible to a Parisian, except for a few local word substitutions (*breuvages* instead of *boissons,* beverages), but the working man's accent and dialect *(joual)* is as far from Parisian French as Cockney is from the Queen's English.

Do you speak English?	**Parlez-vous anglais?**
Good morning/Good day	**Bonjour**
Please	**S'il vous plaît**
Thank you	**Merci**
You're welcome	**Bienvenue**

The Berlitz phrase book, FRENCH FOR TRAVELLERS, covers most situations you're likely to encounter in Montreal. In addition, the Berlitz French-English/English-French pocket dictionary contains a 12,500-word glossary of each language, plus a menu-reader supplement.

LAUNDRY and DRY-CLEANING *(blanchissage; nettoyage à sec)*. All hotels will arrange to have laundry done on weekdays, often with **115**

L same-day service, and some even provide irons and drying lines in the bathroom if you prefer to do your own laundry.

Some Chinese hand laundries are found in the Chinatown district *(quartier chinois)*, centered on Clark and La Gauchetière Streets, and coin-operated laundromats *(buanderie)* function here and there throughout the city.

When will it be ready?	**Quand est-ce que ce sera prêt?**
I must have this for tomorrow morning.	**Il me le faut pour demain matin.**

LOST AND FOUND PROPERTY *(objets trouvés)*; **LOST CHILDREN.** The "lost articles" office for the Metro and city buses is in the Pie IX Metro station; open from 8 a.m. to 1:30 p.m., Monday through Friday (tel.: 877-6006). Otherwise contact the police, tel.: 911.

If your child wanders off in an underground shopping area, the shopkeeper will help you to find him.

I've lost my child/wallet/handbag/passport.	**J'ai perdu mon enfant/portefeuille/sac à main/passeport.**

M **MAIL** *(courrier)*. Have your mail sent either to your hotel or to General Delivery *(poste restante)* care of any post office in Montreal. For the central post office, letters should be addressed thus:

Mr. John Smith
Poste Restante
Station "A"
Montreal, Que. H3C 2HO
Canada

To pick up your mail, go to 1025 Saint-Jacques (St. James) Street West in downtown Montreal, and take some form of identification. For opening hours, see POST OFFICES.

Have you received any mail for...?	**Y a-t-il du courrier pour...?**

MAPS. Good, detailed maps *(plan)* of downtown Montreal, Old Montreal and the Montreal Urban Community as well as an excellent road map *(carte routière)* of the province are available from the Quebec Department of Tourism, Fish and Game office (see TOURIST

INFORMATION OFFICES). *Guide Montréal*, a comprehensive map book and street index is sold at bookstores and some newsstands.

a street plan of...	**un plan de...**
a road map of this region	**une carte routière de cette région**

MEDICAL CARE. See also EMERGENCIES. Large hotels have a nurse on duty and a doctor on call at all times. Hospital emergency rooms, in general, give fast and efficient service. Doctors' fees and hospital care tend to be rather expensive, so you should make sure that your health insurance or health care plan will cover expenses should you become ill in Canada. Alternatively ask your insurance representative, automobile association or travel agent for details of special travel insurance policies. Visitors to Canada may also obtain health insurance coverage from the Ontario Blue Cross, a non-profit organization. Details of the plans, and application forms, may be obtained directly from: Ontario Blue Cross, 150 Ferrand Drive, Don Mills, Ontario M3C 1H6.

Drugstores and chemists' shops *(pharmacie)* have long opening hours (7 a.m. to 10 or 11:30 p.m.). The pharmacy at 1370 Mont Royal Avenue East is open day and night seven days a week (tel.: 527-8827). Consulates and tourist offices can provide lists of recommended doctors and dentists.

I need a doctor/dentist.   **Il me faut un médecin/dentiste.**

MEETING PEOPLE. Language is a hot political issue, and for this reason should be taken seriously. If you do speak French, even if only a smattering, it's really worth doing so with all French Canadians. You may switch to English after a while as being more practical, but you'll have shown them that you did not take their speaking English for granted.

A word on ways to broach a conversation: when asking a stranger for directions, start with *Pardon* (Excuse me) to pave the way; *Bonjour* (Good morning/Good day) is appreciated at all times of the day (Montrealers will even tend to say *Bonjour* when leaving a shop, rather than standard French *Au revoir*).

French-speaking Montrealers tend to observe the little formalities and courtesies more than the English-speakers who share a common, more relaxed and easy-going approach with the Americans. Traditionally, French-speakers tend to keep social life a group activity. English-speaking Montrealers, however, go to pubs and outdoor cafés alone

M or in pairs to meet new people, and the direct, open approach is acceptable, even expected: a person alone in a pub is there to meet new people.

You'll find the Montrealers of all language-groups naturally hospitable and proud of their city's accomplishments.

N **NEWSPAPERS and MAGAZINES** *(journal; revue).* Newsstands in large hotels carry the major French-language Montreal papers as well as the English-language *Gazette* and *Sunday Express,* and often the *New York Times.* The same newsstands may provide you free with the local morning paper of your choice if you fill out an order slip (ask at the reception). Magazines and other newspapers are sometimes carried by hotel newsstands, or can be found in the Central Station under the Queen Elizabeth hotel. A large stand with a very wide-ranging selection is the Metropolitan News on Peel Street between Sainte-Catherine and Dominion Square, open from 8 a.m. till midnight every day. Foreign newspapers usually arrive in Montreal the same day, the London and Paris ones often by mid-morning.

P **PETS**. Cats and dogs entering from the U.S.A. must be accompanied by a certificate signed by a vet certifying the animal has been vaccinated against rabies within the preceding 36 months. Pets from other countries may be subject to special regulations, so it's best to check with a Canadian consulate or information service office before you leave home. On return to Great Britain or Eire, a dog will have to be kept in quarantine for six months; the U.S. reserves the right to quarantine returning animals as well.

Some large hotels permit animals, and may even have special kennels, but it's best to check on their rules in advance.

PHOTOGRAPHY. Purchase and repair of cameras, buying film or having it developed are all easy in Montreal, though a bit more expensive than in the U.S. Camera shops give the fastest service for developing film, though almost any drugstore will do it for you in a week.

I'd like a film for this camera.	**Je voudrais un film pour cette caméra.**
a black-and-white film	**un film en noir et blanc**
a film for color prints	**un film en couleur**
a color-slide film	**un film de diapositives**
How long will it take to develop (and print) this film?	**Combien de temps faudra-t-il pour développer (et tirer) ce film?**

POLICE *(police)*. Of the police forces in Quebec, the federal RCMP
(Royal Canadian Mounted Police) are the most colorful and romantic,
but they are rarely seen except when taking part in ceremonies and
celebrations. Police duties in Montreal are performed by the municipal
MUC (Montreal Urban Community) police force wearing blue uniforms. In addition, a provincial police force, La Sûreté du Québec, in
brown uniforms, patrols highways and provides police service in small
towns and in the countryside. Police emergency number: 911.

Where's the nearest police station?	**Où se trouve le poste de police le plus proche?**

POST OFFICES *(poste)*. See also MAIL, TELEGRAMS and TELEPHONE.
Montreal's central post office is at 1025 Saint-Jacques Street West (tel.:
283-2564). Business hours for post offices are 8 a.m. to 5:45 p.m.
weekdays, 9 a.m. to noon on Saturdays. Postage stamps *(timbre)* can
also be bought in many shops, from vending machines and in hotels.
Mail boxes which are painted red, are located in the streets, in rail and
bus stations and in hotel lobbies, and times of collection are posted on
them.

special delivery (express)	**par exprès**
airmail	**par avion**
general delivery (poste restante)	**poste restante**
A stamp for this letter/ postcard, please.	**Un timbre pour cette lettre/ carte postale, s'il vous plaît.**

PUBLIC HOLIDAYS *(jour férié)*. See also page 89. When a holiday
falls on a Sunday, the following Monday is often observed as the
holiday. These holidays are the official ones, when all government
offices and most businesses are closed:

January 1	*Jour de l'An*	New Year's Day
July 1	*Fête du Canada*	Canada Day
November 11	*Jour de l'Armistice*	Remembrance Day
December 25	*Jour de Noël*	Christmas Day
December 26	*Après-Noël*	Boxing Day

P

Movable dates:	*Vendredi Saint*	Good Friday
	Lundi de Pâques	Easter Monday
Monday before May 25	*Fête de Dollard ou de la Reine*	Fête de Dollard or Victoria Day
First Monday in September	*Fête du travail*	Labor Day
Second Monday in October	*Jour d'Action de grâce*	Thanksgiving Day

In addition, Quebecers observe at least in part:

| June 24 | *Fête de la Saint-Jean-Baptiste* | St. John the Baptist's Day (Patron Saint of French Canadians) |

PUBLIC TRANSPORTATION. The CTCUM/MUCTC *(Commission de Transport de la Communauté Urbaine de Montréal),* Montreal Urban Community Transit Commission, operates the city's bus and Metro systems, which are attractive, clean and highly efficient. Tickets for the system can be bought individually (see p. 103), and transfers between the two systems *(correspondance)* are free. However, tickets good for both bus and Metro are also sold at a small discount in books of six *(carnet de billets)* at newsstands and Metro stations.

It's important you know in which direction you are going, because nearly each bus or Metro line has its own stop or platform. The Metro, for instance, is sometimes on two or three levels.

The **Metro** is modeled on that of Paris, with trains as long as the station platform. When paying to enter the Metro, drop the exact change down the transparent plastic chute in the ticket-seller's booth; if you need change, slip a bill through the hole at the bottom of the booth window. The Metro operates from 5:30 a.m. until 1 a.m.

Bus: For a journey where you want to transfer from bus to Metro, the procedure is the following: board at the front of the bus, pay the exact fare and ask the driver for a transfer. When you switch to the Metro, insert the transfer in the turnstile slot; *another* transfer will be issued for you from the automatic dispenser just inside the turnstiles. After your train journey, you can use this second transfer on a bus; just hand it to the driver. It sounds complicated, but it's all part of the fun. Buses on **120** Sainte-Catherine and Saint-Denis routes operate 24 hours a day.

Maps of the metro network are found on the station walls. For further information, call 288-6287.

RADIO and TV *(radio; télévision)*. Montreal has eight English-language radio stations and the same number of French-language stations (three of each are FM), plus two dual-language FM stations and one multilingual station to serve the city's ethnic minorities. This last station broadcasts in 17 languages.

Six television stations, two English and four French, serve the Montreal area: channels 2 and 6 are run by the Canadian Broadcasting Corporation *(Radio-Canada),* and other channels are private commercial stations. Full details of weekly broadcasting schedules are published as a supplement in Sunday newspapers.

Cable television, widely available, provides some 30 channels, including several from the U.S.

RELIGIOUS SERVICES *(messe; culte)*. Quebec is a predominantly Roman Catholic province. Besides the many Catholic churches, Montreal has churches of all major denominations and some of the smaller ones as well. Anglican/Episcopalian, Baptist, Presbyterian, Pentecostal, Christian Science, Latter-Day Saints and Unitarian are all represented. The city's Jewish temples represent the Reform, Conservative and Orthodox rites. A mosque in Ville Saint-Laurent is the focal point for worship by the city's Muslims.

The large hotels and many smaller ones post a list of churches, with addresses and times of services, and similar lists are published in the Friday *Gazette*. Be sure to check which language the service will be in.

TAXIS *(taxi)*. Several private taxi fleets serve Montreal. The automobiles used are usually American-style sedans, clearly marked as taxis. You'll find taxi stands near the big hotels, in squares and at railroad and bus terminals. The drivers make an effort to be courteous and know their job. Your hotel will have a list of telephone numbers if you prefer to ring for one. All cabs are metered, and rates, plus the driver's name and number, are posted in the car. See also p. 103.

TELEGRAMS *(télégramme)*. Canadian post offices don't handle telegrams. This service is operated by CN-CP (Canadian National-Canadian Pacific) Telecommunications. In Montreal you'll find this office at 360 Saint-Jacques Street West. Telegrams can be phoned in by calling 861-7311.

T   *Téléposte*—where the CN-CP communications network links up with the post distribution service—allows messages to be delivered within a day or less. All you do is to phone in your message to the nearest CN-CP center that transmits it to anywhere within Canada or the U.S.

TELEPHONE *(téléphone)*. The telephone company, Bell Canada, is similar to the U.S. Bell System, so service and procedures are virtually identical in both countries. Directions for pay-phone use are posted beside phones in booths in both French and English. The directories *(annuaire des téléphones)* are White Pages *(Pages Blanches)* containing private, public and government subscribers' numbers and a list of sample long-distance rates; and Yellow Pages *(Pages Jaunes)*, businesses, services and organizations grouped by type, product or service. Long-distance calls, which can be dialed direct, will be station-to-station calls unless you signal the operator (dial zero) and specify person-to-person *(appel de personne-à-personne)*, or collect *(appel à frais virés)*. For overseas calls *(appel à outre-mer)*, dial 0 (zero) and ask for the country you wish to call.

TIME DIFFERENCES. Most of Quebec province, including Montreal and Quebec City, is on Eastern Time, the same as New York and the entire U.S. east coast. Regions farther east (the Gaspé Peninsula, Nova Scotia, New Brunswick) are on Atlantic Time; Newfoundland has its own Newfoundland Time, one half-hour earlier than Atlantic. To the west of Quebec are four more time zones covering the rest of Canada and the U.S.A.: Central, Mountain, Pacific and Yukon. From the last Sunday in April until the last Saturday in October, clocks are advanced one hour to Daylight Saving Time.

Vancouver/ Los Angeles	Winnipeg/ Chicago	New York/ **Montreal**	Halifax	St. John's	London
9 a.m.	11 a.m.	**noon**	1 p.m.	1.30 p.m.	5 p.m.

What time is it, please?   **Quelle heure est-il, s'il vous plaît?**

TIPPING. Since a service charge is normally not included in hotel and restaurant bills, tipping is customary. It is also appropriate to give something extra to bellboys, hat-check attendants, etc., for their services. The chart below gives some suggestions as to how much to leave.

Hairdresser/Barber	15%
Maid, per day	$1.50
Porter, per bag	75¢
Taxi driver	15%
Tour guide	10% (optional)
Waiter	15%

TOILETS *(toilettes)*. In this bilingual city where more and more signs bear symbols, not words, almost all toilets have the familiar pictographs of a man or a woman, although you may encounter the words *Hommes* (Men) and *Dames* (Ladies). Department stores, rail and bus stations and many underground complexes have public toilets, but they are few and far between, so take advantage of what you find.

Where are the toilets, please?   **Où sont les toilettes, s'il**
                                    vous plaît?

TOURIST INFORMATION OFFICES *(renseignements touristiques)*. The Canadian Government Office of Tourism and the Quebec Department of Tourism maintain information offices in many foreign countries. They'll supply you with informative brochures, maps and hotel guides. Ask for a copy of Montreal's *Calendar of Events*, a seasonal list published four times a year with information on scheduled art exhibitions, theater, concerts, sports and special events.

Some addresses of Quebec or Canadian Government offices abroad:

Australia: Canadian Government Office of Tourism, 8th floor, AMP Centre, 50 Bridge Street, *Sydney* 2000; tel.: 231-6522.

Great Britain: Délégation Générale du Québec, 59 Pall Mall, *London* SW1Y SJH; tel.: (01) 930-8314.

Canadian Government Office of Tourism, Canada House, Trafalgar Square, *London* SW1Y 5BJ; tel.: 629-9492.

U.S.A.: Délégation Générale du Québec, 17 W. 50th Street, Rockefeller Center, *New York,* NY 10020; tel.: (212) 397-0200.

Délégation du Québec, Exchange Place, 19th floor, 53 State St., *Boston,* MA 02109; tel.: (617) 723-3366.

Délégation du Québec, 700 S. Flower St., Suite 1520, *Los Angeles,* CA 90017; tel.: (213) 689-4861.

T   In Montreal, both the Quebec Government and the Montreal Urban Community maintain tourist information offices:

Quebec Department of Tourism, Fish and Game: 2 Place Ville-Marie; tel.: (514) 873-2015. Open seven days a week from 9 a.m. to 5 p.m. (from 9 a.m. to 9 p.m. in the summer).

Municipal Tourist Office: 174 Notre-Dame Street East; tel.: (514) 871-1595. Open from 8:30 a.m. to 4:30 p.m., Monday through Friday.

There are also tourist information offices at Dorval and Mirabel airports.

TRAINS *(train)*. See also INTERCITY BUSES. VIA Rail Canada, an Amtrak-like quasi-public corporation, operates all passenger services in Canada, using lines, stations and equipment of what used to be Canadian National and Canadian Pacific railroads.

For information and schedules, call:

VIA Rail Canada 871-1331.

Note: Canrailpasses are available for Europeans, giving unlimited rail travel for periods of 8, 15, 22 or 30 days at a flat rate. They must be bought in Europe before departure. Ask your travel agent for details.

W   **WATER** *(eau)*. All tap water is safe to drink. Luxury hotels often have ice water taps in bathrooms, and most hotels and motels provide ice, usually from an ice-making machine placed in the corridor or stairwell. Well-known brands of Canadian and French mineral water are sold in specialty groceries and in better restaurants.

a bottle of mineral water	**une bouteille d'eau minérale**
carbonated/non-carbonated	**gazeuse/non gazeuse**

Y   **YOUTH HOSTELS** *(auberge de jeunesse)*. The Canadian Hostelling Association publishes a quarterly newspaper called *Hosteller/l'Ajiste,* with a directory of all the youth hostels in Canada as well as information on tours, bicycle trips, skiing, charter flights and the like. They also issue International Membership Cards. Contact:

Canadian Hostelling Association, National Office, 333 River Road, Vanier City (Ottawa), Ont. K1L 8B9; tel.: (613) 746-0060.

Headquarters of the Quebec Province branch of the CHA are at 3541 Aylmer Street, Montreal H2X 2B9; tel.: (514) 843-3317.

SOME USEFUL EXPRESSIONS

yes/no	**oui/non**
please/thank you	**s'il vous plaît/merci**
excuse me	**excusez-moi**
you're welcome	**bienvenue**
where/when/how	**où/quand/comment**
how long/how far	**combien de temps/à quelle distance**
yesterday/today/tomorrow	**hier/aujourd'hui/demain**
day/week/month/year	**jour/semaine/mois/année**
left/right	**gauche/droite**
up/down	**en haut/en bas**
good/bad	**bon/mauvais**
big/small	**grand/petit**
cheap/expensive	**bon marché/cher**
hot/cold	**chaud/froid**
old/new	**vieux/neuf**
open/closed	**ouvert/fermé**
Does anyone here speak English?	**Y a-t-il quelqu'un ici qui parle anglais?**
What does this mean?	**Que signifie ceci?**
I don't understand.	**Je ne comprends pas.**
Please write it down.	**Veuillez bien me l'écrire.**
Is there an admission charge?	**Y a-t-il des frais d'entrée?**
Waiter!/Waitress!	**Garçon!/Mademoiselle!**
I'd like...	**J'aimerais...**
How much is that?	**C'est combien?**
Have you something less expensive?	**Avez vous quelque chose de meilleur marché?**
What time is it?	**Quelle heure est-il?**
Help me please.	**Aidez-moi, s'il vous plaît.**
Get a doctor—quickly!	**Un médecin, vite!**

Index

An asterisk (*) next to a page number indicates a map reference.

088/906 RPC 12